I0071732

How To Raise Your First Million Dollars From Angel Investors

Volume 1 (second edition)

An Insiders Look At Some Of The Leading

Angel Investor Groups In America

FundingPost.com

© 2009 FundingPost (A Second Venture Corporation)

ISBN 978-0-578-02627-5

<u>ACKNOWLEDGEMENTS</u>

FundingPost would like to thank:

- Mark Butterworth, Ohio Tech Angels, OH
- Bharat Chandria, Ohio Tech Angels, OH
- Jeff Cohn, Tech Coast Angels, CA
- Denis Coleman, Band of Angels, CA
- Lou Anne Flanders-Stec, Piedmont Angel Network, NC
- Nicola Foreman, Band of Angels, CA
- Tom Grant, Richmond Venture Forum, VA
- Rusty Griffith, Maryland Angels Council, MD
- Garrett Hunter, Cherrystone Angel Group, RI
- John Huston, Ohio Tech Angels, OH
- Neil McLean, Angel Investor, SC
- Catherine Mott, BlueTree Allied Angels, PA
- Robert J. Robinson, University of Hawaii Angels, HI
- Ellen Sandles, Tri-State Private Investors' Network, NY
- Chris Saxman *(fmr)*, New York Angels, NY
- Charles Sidman, Maine Angels, ME
- Chris Starr, Innovation Philadelphia and MAG Fund, PA
- Steve Stephansen, Sand Hill Angels, CA
- David Weaver, Great Lakes Angels, MI
- Rick Wolk, Alaska InvestNET, AK
- Bruce Woodry, Aurora Angels, MI
- Richard Anders, Mass Medical Angels, MA
- Dee Harris, Arizona Angels, AZ

FundingPost would also to thank Judy Rubin for editing and Deborah Hertlein for updating the new edition.

ABOUT FUNDINGPOST

For over nine years FundingPost has worked with thousands of Angel and Venture Capital Investors and Entrepreneurs. With over 8,000 CEOs and 500 Venture Funds attending events in 19 cities nationwide, a quarterly Dealflow magazine, and a deal-exchange Website that has, on average, seen an introduction of an Investor to an Entrepreneur every business day since its inception, FundingPost believes that it is important to reach investors in every medium possible – both online and offline, and it is still experiencing strong growth despite current economic conditions. Please check out our website at www.FundingPost.com for more information about our online deal-exchange and event schedule. For more information about FundingPost products, including audio and video files of previous events and e-books on angel and venture capital investing, please go to: www.FundingPost.com

ABOUT THE AUTHOR

Aren Cohen joined FundingPost in 2004 as Vice President of Business Development . Aren's responsibilities at FundingPost included product development, affiliate and investor relations and event promotion.

Before joining FundingPost, Aren spent two years working as a venture capitalist at Scripps Ventures, where she focused primarily on investments in the education industry. In addition, Aren has also worked in various financial capacities at the Guggenheim Museum, CBS, Inc., and two start-up companies, Skoodles, Inc., and Concrete Media Construction, and has served as a consultant to start-up businesses. Aren holds a Bachelor of Arts magna cum laude from Harvard University, and her Master's of Business Administration is from New York University's Stern School of Business._

TABLE OF CONTENTS

Welcome to **How To Raise Your First Million Dollars (Volume 1) -** In this brief we present 10 interviews with leading Angel Groups and Angel Investors across the country. Why did we see the need for this book? In 2004, FundingPost held five events in New York, Philadelphia, Washington, DC, Seattle and Silicon Valley focused on Angel Investing. These events were held in packed rooms— it was clear to us that there is a huge demand on the part of entrepreneurs to meet and to learn successful tactics to attract Angel Investors. As of 2009, FundingPost has organized over 150 consistently sold-out Angel Investor and Venture Capitalist events in 17 cities across the United States. Yet along with our events, it became clear to us that there was a demand for more. How could we bring our FundingPost entrepreneurs more information about Angel Investors? We decided that we should let the Angels speak for themselves. So we compiled this collection of conversations with Angel Investors and this book was born! In this introduction, we will provide you with some background on Angel Investors and also the highlights and themes of our interviews. Then read on and see what the Angels themselves say, what they invest in and why they continue to invest .Enjoy and happy fundraising!

> **TIP:** A SERIAL ENTREPRENEUR is a person who has a successful track record of starting companies and taking them to profitability. Serial entrepreneurs are often people with lots of ideas who want to start companies, but have little interest in actually managing and running them once they are going concerns. They like the creativity and challenge of start-up environments.

The process of Angel investing, the process in which wealthy individuals make highly speculative investments in early-stage companies, has been around for many years; even Alexander Graham Bell was funded by Angel Investors in 1874.[1] In general, the average Angel Investor is someone who was himself an

---

[1] Van Osnabrugge, M. and Robinson, R., "Angel Investing: Matching Start-Up Funds with Start-Up Companies," Jossey-Bass, Inc.: San Francisco, 2004. pg. 41.

entrepreneur, or even a **serial entrepreneur.** Often at retirement age, he realizes the value of keeping part of his portfolio in high-risk investments and also wants to "keep his hand in the game." His previous career allows the Angel to bring knowledge and resources to his investment, and many times Angels invest (solely) in industries and technologies in which they have prior experience. Often an Angel will invest approximately $25K-50K in a first round of a deal, and he may expect to contribute in later rounds of fundraising. In addition, Angels often want to be actively involved with their investments, and they tend to invest locally or regionally.

However, in the last 10 years this process of Angel investing has changed and become much more organized. Previously, Angel Investors tended to work alone and find opportunities by themselves. Now, more recently, there has been a growing trend that has resulted in the formation of Angel "groups." From 1996 to 2004, the number of Angel Groups in the U.S. grew from 10 to approximately 200.[2] This phenomenal growth is a testament to the increased opportunity for Angel investing, as well as proof that Angel Investors have come to understand the value of pooling resources and strategic intelligence. In 2003, The Ewing Marion Kauffman Foundation (www.kauffman.org) funded the creation of the Angel Capital Association (www.angelcapitalassociation.org), in response to research from its four "Angel Organization Summits." This group's charter states that its mission is to "support activities for the advancement of angel investing and angel investment groups."[3] Specifically, the organization exists to assist the field of Angel investing in

---

[2] Preston, Susan L., Esq. "Angel Investment Groups, Networks, and Funds: A Guidebook to Developing the Right Angel Organization for Your Community." The Ewing Marion Kauffman Foundation, August 2004. www.kauffman.org/pdf/angel_guidebook.pdf

[3] Angel Capital Association Charter. www.angelcapitalassociation.org/downloads/about/Overview_ACACharter.pdf

the following ways: 1. Define angel investing and angel investing organizations, 2. Advocate angel investing with entrepreneurs and equity investors and 3. Promote the establishment of angel organizations.[4]

These Angel Groups provide a wonderful opportunity for entrepreneurs because they offer a structured enviroRAent in which to seek capital and access to many potential investors. These Angel Groups take many forms, some being no more than a loose association of individuals, while others, like the Band of Angels in California, are highly-organized investment clubs that sometimes have their own funds alongside the monies each individual Angel may contribute. These groups are beneficial because they provide an access point for entrepreneurs and they often allow Angels to share intelligence and responsibilities for making an investment. These groups tend to be highly regional, with the Cherrystone Angel Group of Rhode Island focusing on deals from Rhode Island, Connecticut and Massachusetts, while the University of Hawaii Angels expect all of their deals to have an interest in Hawaii.

Angel Groups source their deals in many ways. Most notably, members of the networks often see deals that they bring to the group, and this is by far the most preferred method of sourcing a deal. The interviews revealed that Angel Groups have a preference for deals that come to them from a known, trusted source because that provides a first screen, offering an early endorsement. In addition, many groups have associations with professional organizations including law firms and accounting firms, investment banks and Venture Capitalists that refer deals to the Angel Groups. In some cases, the Angel Networks also have relationships with university research labs, **incubators** and other trusted sources such as FundingPost which funnel dealflow. Finally, many of

---

[4] ibid

these groups have websites where an entrepreneur can submit his or her Executive Summary for consideration.

> **TIP:** INCUBATORS are organizations that offer resources for start-up companies. Commonly found in urban centers and university environments, incubators can provide things like office space and administrative support. Incubators often support multiple companies at the same time in the same space, thus, offering these young companies a sense of community and camaraderie along with the other more tangible resources they provide.

Once a deal has made it into the hands of an Angel Group, it still has a long way to go before an investment is made. Based on our conversations and research, it seems like most Angel Networks are averaging about three to five investments per year. Granted there are some exceptions to that, particularly in the older, more established groups with more resources like Band of Angels, who have done as many as nine deals in a year. But, for the most part, the groups are not only highly selective but they also have limited bandwidth for how many deals they can actually do. In addition, the average investment size for these groups tends to be around $250K-500K, with the occasional exception where the investment can climb to upwards of $1M+.

The screening process for evaluating deals has become highly evolved for the more senior groups, and many of the young Angel Networks seem to be emulating these processes. The Kauffman research has found that a tiered screening process is a best practice.[5] After a staff member or volunteer reads through a business plan and gives it an initial

---

[5] Preston, Susan L., Esq. "Angel Investment Groups, Networks, and Funds: A Guidebook to Developing the Right Angel Organization for Your Community." The Ewing Marion Kauffman Foundation, August 2004. www.kauffman.org/pdf/angel_guidebook.pdf

ok, many of these groups have CEOs come in for a meeting to do a brief (15-minute) pitch to a screening committee of Angel members. Based on a consensus of opinion, that group may decide to do either more research or move directly to bring the investment to a larger meeting of the entire network. Once the pitching company has reached a meeting of full membership, the group will decide if the company should move into **due-diligence**. Often due-diligence will be led either by a "champion" Angel or team of Angels, generally with experience in the company's given industry. The Angels we spoke to said that often the initial screening process (to meeting the full Angel Membership) usually took two months, and the due-diligence process could take anywhere from weeks to several months, depending on how far along and well prepared a company was.

> **TIP:** DUE-DILIGENCE is the name of the intense and rigorous process when investors do their research on a company in order to decide if they should invest. Due-diligence is sort of like an "engagement period" before a company and an Angel "get married." During due-diligence, a potential investor will examine the background and credit histories of management, review all contracts that a company holds, examine all financial and legal documents, etc. Due-diligence is a critical part of the investment process because it gives the Angel the confidence that he knows all the details about the investment he is going to make.

So, if you are an entrepreneur, what are the key factors that will drive an Angel to invest in your company? In our conversations with Angels and Angel Group coordinators, we learned that there are five main areas that are critical for securing investment. These are: 1. Business Plan/Executive Summary; 2. Market size and competitive landscape; 3. Intellectual property; 4. Management team; and 5. Customer base.

1.   Business Plan/Executive Summary: Angel investors are looking for business plans and executive summaries that are clear, concise and to the point. They want to be able to understand your business quickly. As one Angel put it, "Tell me what you do." In a more fully realized business plan, there is the expectation that the entrepreneur will present the background of the management team, a marketing plan, information about the competitive landscape and reasonable financial statements. However, the message that came out most clearly was: "Keep it short and simple."

2.   Market Size and Competitive Landscape: Market size is important to Angel Investors. Angels are looking for big returns on every investment with the understanding that not every investment will provide huge returns, but in an overall portfolio there should be a respectable overall return. As a result, many Angels told us that they are not looking for **"Lifestyle businesses".** If you are planning to start a small business that will make $2M-5M a year, Angels are not an appropriate source for capital. Angels want to invest in companies that will grow to $10M-50M in revenue in three to seven years.   Hence, they choose to invest in high-growth

> **TIP:** A LIFESTYLE BUSINESS, often a family business, is a profitable business that will have a steady stream of revenues and make up to roughly $5M a year. Unlike Angel-backed businesses, they are not "rapid" (i.e., $50M in revenue in five years) growth companies. While lifestyle businesses can be very successful enterprises, they are not the deals Angels are looking for because they will not provide a large enough economic reward.

industries like Information Technology (software, hardware, Internet, nanotechnology), the Life Sciences (biotechnology, medical devices), Real Estate and even Agriculture. In addition, Angels expect that entrepreneurs understand the market in which they will be operating and have a good sense of the competition in the space. Angels do not expect a company to exist without competition, but they want their entrepreneurs to have a strategy that involves, understands and, perhaps, even partners or eventually sees an exit strategy that involves its competitors. An exit strategy is important. Remember that Angel Investors are in this to make money, as well!

3.   Intellectual Property: Angels do not always require patents, although they do acknowledge that in some cases patents or patents pending are an attractive addition to a deal. They do expect that a company have some sort of defensible intellectual property, either in the form of patents or trade secrets that will create a significant **barrier-to-entry** for competitors.

> **TIP:** A BARRIER-TO-ENTRY is the unique product or process that is difficult to replicate, giving a company an unfair competitive advantage in the marketplace. Barriers-to-entry include: Resource ownership, patents or copyright, governmental restrictions or high start-up costs. Any of these factors give a company a real advantage in the marketplace because they prevent other companies from easily copying and manufacturing the same product, thus, creating a monopolistic and advantageous situation for the holder of the barrier-to-entry.

4.   Management Team: There is no question that the management team of an entrepreneurial venture is an essential component of an Angel's consideration. Every Angel we spoke to made mention of the importance of a strong

management team. The definition of a "strong management team" included a seasoned entrepreneur (often defined as a "serial entrepreneur" who had already succeeded in another venture) who has a deep knowledge and ideally strong connections within the given industry. Most Angels acknowledged that the full management team might not be in place, but they wanted to see that the entrepreneur would have appropriate people tapped to come on board when the time was right. Angels talked about wanting to see a "mature" team capable of selling. As one interviewee astutely pointed out, "An entrepreneur has to do a lot of selling; selling to future employees, selling to partners and customers... it is important that an entrepreneur knows how to sell." In addition, it was important to Angels that entrepreneurs know their gaps and how to fill them. This could take many forms, in terms of an **Advisory Board** with talent to assist and help make connections; it could also mean people who have been tapped to come on board. Also, they want to understand the depth of an entrepreneur's relationships and his knowledge of an industry.

5.   Customers: Along with the management team, customers were the most important factor that would influence an Angel to invest. It is very important to investors to see that there is a market need for the product and that there are people who are willing to buy and use the solution a company is presenting. If there are no potential customers, it is difficult to accept the proof of concept. In the most ideal situation, Angels would like to see paying customers using the product. If the company is not in that stage, they want to see alpha or beta

trials, or at least be able to speak to people who are in the pipeline ready to adopt the product when it is ready. Even in pre-revenue companies, Angels want to be able to talk to people who will validate the need for the product. As Denis Coleman of Band of Angels put it, there has to be at least a "Free Test," where someone might not even be willing to pay for the solution, but they will say that they will use the product

> **TIP:** AN ADVISORY BOARD is a group of individuals, often with experience in a given industry, who offer counsel to a company. Unlike a Board of Directors, individuals on an Advisory Board generally do not have an economic interest in the company. An Advisory Board can offer connections, insights and advice that will help an entrepreneur grow his company in directions that will help secure financing and fuel revenue growth.

if it was given to them for free.

So once an Angel decides that it is worthwhile to invest in the deal, how does he decide on a **valuation** for the deal. Angel Investor, Neil McLean called valuation at this stage "a black art." Most Angels spoke of valuations as a process of a combination of factors. Certainly, all of the considerations

> **TIP:** WHAT IS A VALUATION? This is the amount of money that investors think the company is worth. Generally, there are a "pre-money" and a "post-money" valuation. Say an Angel values a deal at $1M, and he plans to invest $500K. The "pre-money" for that deal would be the $1M value and 100% equity held by the original investors before the Angel makes his investment. Once the Angel makes his investment, the "post-money" valuation of the deal would be $1.5M. Now 66.6% of the equity would be owned by the original investors and 33.3% of the equity would be held by the Angel.

discussed above, business plan, market size and competitive landscape, intellectual property, management team and customer base, are essential elements that will impact valuation. Most importantly, Angels want to see how far along a company is with respect to those five elements. The farther along, the more valuable the deal is. In addition, Angels usually see a lot of deals and keep up with other deals being done in an industry, so they use their knowledge of other deals as comparables for setting the value on an investment. Finally,

TIP: OPTIONS OR WARRANTS is a feature written into term sheets that allows an investor to acquire additional shares in the next round of funding at a discounted price to the valuation of the new round. In other words, let's say Company X is going into its second round of funding and the new investors are valuing the company at $15M post-money. In the previous round the Angel Investor had invested a bridge note of $1M with warrants for another $.5M to buy stock at $2/share. The new investor has decided that the $15M post-money is based on a total of 5M shares, or $3/share. In this new round, the Angel would be able buy an additional 1M shares for $1M, whereas the new investor will buy 1M shares for $1.5M. This is an advantage for the Angel Investor because he can increase his investment in the next round, allowing him to increase his percentage of ownership in the company at a discounted price, which will allow him to receive a greater return when the company reaches its exit.

TIP: COMPARABLES are the values of other deals being done of similar size and stage in the same or similar industries. In other words, if you were looking to value a store like Target, you might also want to look at the financial results of KMart, Sears and Wal-Mart. Comparables are helpful because they put revenues and exit multiples into the context of the market and they are used to benchmark the value of a deal.

Angels will evaluate projected financial cash flows and apply some appropriate discount rate to account for risk, and use that as a benchmark for valuation.

It is worth noting that while Venture Capitalists often favor discounted cash flows and comparables as the best way to value a deal, most Angels tend to use the first measure of "How far along are you?" as the primary method of valuation. Often

comparables and projected cash flows are viewed as too unpredictable to be a solid measure of valuation, so the "black art" of "gut feeling" plays a large part in Angel valuations. Most of the Angels we spoke to said current valuations are coming in around $1M-3M. Valuation can often be a sticking point to Angel deals, and Angels want entrepreneurs to be open to creating fair equity structures. Angels explained that if management cannot trust an Angel on valuation that it does not bode well for the working relationship going forward. So it is best for an entrepreneur to be open and partner with an Angel with a valuation he trusts.

When an Angel sets a valuation, what are his expectations for the deal? In terms of an exit, most Angels said that they like a company to come to them with a stated exit strategy of either a plan for an **initial public offering (IPO)** or a **merger or acquisition (M&A).**

If the company plans for an M&A exit, an Angel would like the company to have at least some sense of what companies might be likely acquisition candidates. On average, most Angels expect that it will take three to five years before a liquidity event. And in life sciences, this exit could take

> **TIP:** AN INITIAL PUBLIC OFFERING happens when a company goes to the public markets to raise capital. IPOs were really hot during the "bubble" of the late '90s. When a company issues an initial public offering, they offer shares in the company that will be traded on a major stock exchange. Once the shares are in the public market, they will trade at a value set by the marketplace based on the perceived

> **TIP:** A MERGER OR ACQUISITON happens when two companies join together. In the case of a merger, the combination of the two companies is considered a "combining of equals." In the case of an acquisition, one company is considered to be buying out another. In the case of a merger or acquisition, the price of the acquired company is mutually agreed upon by the two parties and is decided privately, based on market information. Generally speaking, it is not required that the price of a merger or acquisition be made public unless one of the parties is itself traded publicly.

closer to seven years because of trials and FDA approvals. Over this time horizon, most Angels want to see a return of 10 times their money. This 10x return may seem aggressive, but put into the context of a larger portfolio, it makes sense. Angels and Angel Group funds often take risks on multiple companies, and they understand that while occasionally one will "hit big," some will fail and others will perform in the middle of the pack. An Angel must assume that each investment will be very successful in order to balance out the underperformers in his portfolio.

> **TIP:** A LEAD INVESTOR sets the valuation of the round and is generally responsible for conducting the majority of the due-diligence on a potential investment. A lead investor is often the champion on a deal and may well have industry knowledge that has made it easier for that person to do in-depth due-diligence. Often other investors will follow the lead based on their knowledge of and trust in the lead investor's experience and reputation as a credible source and investor.

In terms of an overall portfolio performance, most investors want to see three to five times their money in the same number of years.

Angels can choose multiple ways to invest. In some cases, they might serve as the **lead investor**, and sometimes they will follow a syndicate into a deal. Generally, it is the older Angel funds in New York, California and Boston that are most equipped to lead a deal, although other younger groups have also served as lead. Angels might follow other Angels into deals, and in some cases Angels might add on in a round led by Venture Capitalists.

There tend to be two types of term sheets being written for deals these days. The first is a traditional equity term sheet, where an Angel would have a certain amount of stock, often "Preferred A" stock, in the company. In this case, a valuation for the deal was set and the Angel will have favorable liquidation preference based on the class of stock. Angels might also choose to invest using "Bridge Notes" or "Convertible

Notes," often with options or warrants attached. When an Angel invests using a note structure, it means that they will let the Venture Capitalists set the value of the company in the next round of funding. Again, the notes will allow Angels to have liquidation preference, and the warrants will help prevent the Angel from getting overly diluted in the next round. When Angels invest, they will sometimes request a Board seat, usually in line with their being a lead investor. However, even if an Angel hasn't taken a Board seat, Angels, and particularly Angels with industry experience, tend to be actively involved with their investments.

> **TIP:** DILUTION is the process where additional shares of a company are issued so the value of all the shares decreases because more investors are sharing the value of the company.

So, now armed with this information about Angels, what are the best ways to succeed in attracting their investment? We thought the best way to close would be to summarize the highlights of their "one key piece of advice" for entrepreneurs. Below, please find the most important pieces of advice they had to offer. Then read the interviews and learn all the ins and outs for each of the Angels and Angel Group Administrators we spoke to so you'll be fully prepared when it comes time to raise capital for your company!

TIPS FROM THE PROs

- **Know Your Business**: "Have a very realistic understanding of why <your> business is going to make money." Chris Saxman

- **Prove the Concept**: "Really show that you have a business before going out to raise money...Prove the concept." Ellen Sandles

- **Take Advice**: "Be "coach-able" and in that "coach-ability" you've got to build realism – be realistic." Lou Anne Flanders-Stec

- **Know When to Raise Your Capital**: "It's such a full-time position and it requires so much energy and you have to put so many other things on hold while you are fundraising... it's critical you do it at the right time." Nicola Foreman

- **Know your Investor**: "Don't go blindly looking for capital and taking the first dollar that seems interesting... Look at what they've invested in, in the past, and look at where those companies are today." Rusty Griffith

- **Focus on the Investor**: "Spend as much time discussing why it's a good investment as you do explaining why it's a good product." Neil McLean

- **Find a Lead Investor**: "Getting that person to stand forward who has some reputation as an investor or domain knowledge in the field is going to be critical." Dennis Coleman

- **Valuation**: "I would say, don't get too hung up on valuation because at the end of the day it doesn't matter as much as you think it does." Robert Robinson

- **Raise Enough Money**: "Raise enough money to get to a funding milestone, whatever that might be for the company. So they have to be careful not to raise too little money and run out of it... enough money that it can get them to the point in development of the company that another round of capital would be able to be raised to continue scaling the company." Chris Starr

- **Patience is a Virtue**: "You are going to have to realize you are going to have to talk to a lot of people... to raise money." Tom Grant

Nicola Foreman, Deal Manager

Band of Angels Management, LLC

Menlo Park, CA

www.bankangles.com

info@bandangels.com

bond

OF ANGELS

FP: What is the background on the Band of Angels and how did you get interested in Angel investing?

NF: Oh, absolutely. Well, the Band of Angels was started in 1994 and it was funded by Hans Severiens, and Hans had really seen a need within the early investment community for individuals to kind of come together in a collective fashion and lend support to young entrepreneurial organizations before their first round of venture capital. And so to do that, he actually got together with some of his friends at the time who were all ex-management members of successful entrepreneurial organizations themselves, and formed at the time a club that he later called Band of Angels. Band of Angels is kind of the first and foremost Angel organization in the US.

My own background, I actually started out on the other side of the fence. I decided I was going to go work for the wonderful world of start-ups, which I enjoyed immensely. But in doing that I quickly learned that as a start-up pretty much everyone's full prime responsibility was in helping raise money, and so I was quickly involved in really the investor relation side of things. That was my first taste of investing. I went on to do some time over at CS Boston as a marketing analyst, and then circled back into the venture community at an organization called Propelled Partners, before joining up with ENCBSC at the end.

FP: So tell me, what industries does the Band of Angels generally invest in?

NF: Well, if you take a look at kind of our last year's round of investments, which we did nine new investments, 10 follow-on investments, the breakdown actually ended up being about 25% of the deals were done in software, 25% in telecom, about 37.5% were actually done in life sciences. We are very diversified in the industries that we look at and there isn't really one industry that we don't have experience in backing, even down to semi-conductor and consumer. But we tend to, because we have 110 members right now, have a really good split across the deals we look at and the deals we actually invest in.

FP: What is the typical size of investment?

NF: It's about $450K right now.

FP: On average, how many companies are you investing in per year?

NF: The last two years it has been nine companies each year. We actually present 33, very high return. We were actually named #7 last year for top 10 venture capital funds in the US. That's in terms of active deals. And I would anticipate that we are going to go ahead and make that ranking again this year.

FP: How do you look for deals?

NF: We have a varied source of where we would receive our deals, what with the universities—a lot of them come through that way. All of our members are naturally tapped into the entrepreneurial communities, so a large portion of our dealflow comes through our own members. Beyond that, we also have very strong relationships with most of the venture community, so if the deal is too early for one of our VC partner firms to do, they will often send it to us to take a look at and see if we will support them at their young stage. And then there is also, I would say 50% or so of the dealflow that is actually unsolicited, so it's entrepreneurs, it's young start-ups that have looked out there to see who is investing in their space, and have come across Band.

FP: What is the process by which you evaluate a company?

NF: When a company first comes to us typically they will send us their executive summary or business plan at that stage. We have currently 27 members who are a part of our pre-screen process. These 27 members are divided by their industry expertise. Usually, it requires at least six reviewers to take a look at a deal before we decide whether or not we will accept it into the next stage or decline it at that pass. We are looking for all of the same elements that most of the other VC firms are: A strong team, strong technology, a good market opportunity, reasonable capital expectations, strong financials, and those types of things. Once the initial evaluation has been done, which is just a paper pass, we will then invite the top six companies for that month to meet with our screening committee. The screening committee is actually made up of seven members currently. Members are split by chair and then our managing member sits on the seventh chair of the screening committees. They will meet with each of those six companies in a very short meeting and select the top three there to actually come in and present at the next Band of Angels dinner meeting. At that stage, they typically run through a full pitch and after that we will collect RSVPs for follow-up meetings and hopefully, begin due-diligence with the appropriate companies.

FP: How long is that process to the screening dinner and how long does due- diligence usually take?

NF: The nice thing about being an Angel organization is we do have the ability of moving a little bit quicker. That being said, the average deal, to get to the dinner, it takes about six weeks from the first time that we see it on paper to actually meeting with the company to getting them to present to the dinner. As far as an investment post-dinner is concerned, the quickest that I've personally seen it happen is about 3 ½ weeks, and the average is six weeks. So from beginning to end you're really looking at about a 12-week cycle.

FP: What do you look for in a business plan or an executive summary? What would sell you on something?

NF: What we are really looking for there is an entrepreneur who is on to something new or stands out in one particular area. So, for example, if he's got a great success rate in the past, that's a natural inclination for us to believe that they are going to be able to do it again. Team is always critical; no matter, I think, who you are talking to, that's one of the primary areas that we'll look at. The market opportunity also has to be right; we need to know that if we invest in this company that there is really a true market out there for them in the foreseeable future. We don't want to be too early, we don't want to be too late, and so the timing is really critical. Beyond that, the technology, how defensible it is, and of course, some of the other standards will come into play, financials and the capital, like we talked about.

FP: You talked about defensible technology. Do you require that companies have patents?

NF: Not necessarily. I think being defensible isn't solely reliant on patents. Naturally, if you are in the life sciences, biotech or semi industry it should probably be patent defensible. But if you start looking at software and even some of the communications companies, patents really are not all that protectable at the end of the day. What we are really looking for there is an overall defensible strategy, and intellectual property comes in many areas and sometimes you can go ahead and put a patent around it, and sometimes it's better to have a stronger strategy in the long run, such as first mover advantage, ways that you are going to stay ahead of competition in the long run.

FP: What do you expect the entrepreneur to know about the competitive landscape?

NF: Naturally there are going to be some start-ups they are not aware about that may be real, but they should be very, very knowledgeable about the competition. I think one of the biggest fallacies that we see young start-ups make all the time is claiming there is no competition in their space. Every single company out there has a competitor, at least one, and if it isn't Microsoft or one of the big boys then they probably could easily move into their space. And I think it's naïve for a lot of the start-ups to kind of look out there and not take that into consideration. Everything that we do in the investment world, whether you are an Angel Investor or whether you are a tier one VC, really relies heavily on the creditability of the entrepreneur that you are meeting with, and so you have to acknowledge and have to be ready for them to say, We know who the competition is today and we anticipate who the competition is likely to be tomorrow.

FP: What are you looking for in a management team?

NF: Strong backgrounds from the founding team on the operations side. They need to have been immersed in the industry for many years, and typically, if they haven't got that experience, we expect them to have surrounded themselves with people who have. Even if they can't afford it yet because they are young, the first-time CEO is to have the understanding and the expertise to go get an advisory board that has been there and done that and to get the advisory board to buy into what they are doing. So if they, as

I say, don't have their own experience, and it should be in the operations side of things, then we certainly are expecting to see them put a team together that has got that experience.

FP: So even if they are not fully fleshed out they should have resources to get there?

NF: Exactly! Exactly! That is kind of back to that credible issue of knowing where your weak spots are. And I think, as a start-up, no matter how experienced you are, you really are looking for good advice at that stage because there are so many areas you can go into and some pitfalls that you need to avoid. And the only way you are going to do that is really having a strong internal and external team that can help you watch out for those mistakes.

FP: So, what sort of milestones do you expect the company to have reached before investment, and when you make an investment what stage do you expect that money to take them to?

NF: It really kind of depends on the industry that we are talking about. I can speak in generalities inasmuch as a company needs to have validated the market opportunity. We don't want them out there building technology without really knowing that a market opportunity exists. We have references that we can follow up on and, ideally, a reference that is going to be a potential customer down the line. Beyond that we are also looking for the basics, as much as what they have created to date, whether that's a patent, a pending patent portfolio or even just corporate label work. People that we can say, "They came to us at this stage and here is what they have done so far." So ways that we can see they've had past milestones which they have achieved and future milestones which are realistic. As far as what the money should accomplish, if they are coming to us at alpha, we expect them to be able to get to beta. If they are coming to us post-beta, really at the revenue stage, then we need to know that the next round of funding that they are seeking from VCs is likely, and so a lot of the time that's really a matter of hitting the numbers, hitting the revenue marks that they have already laid out for themselves.

FP: When a company comes to you, do you expect them to have a stated exit strategy?

NF: Well, yes, either IPO or acquisition. It's one of those tricky questions; you should probably have an answer to it. There's not really one, the right one, to choose. If they are coming to us with an acquisition play and acknowledging that they expect an early exit in a couple of years through acquisition, then it's nice to have them already have told us who it is that they anticipate. This would be an acquisition for, and certainly, if initial discussions have already been made with those players, that is even better.

FP: What, in general, is the time horizon to the liquidity event and what's the general expected ROI?

NF: The typical exit, again buying licenses by a tech investment, we know that we are in it for the long haul, because playing at the Angel level you have to be, and so five to seven years is the typical average which we will look at. Some of our exits have occurred much earlier. In fact, a couple of the ones last year were literally under two years. But that's not the norm for us. As far as a return, I could tell you that the average return for our investments, and again, just looking at last year's statistics, turned out to be 300%. But we have also had some very high successes that have been more around the 1200% mark, so we are looking for probably - a safe guess is always a 5X return. We have to look at this in terms of the portfolio and the investment. And of course there are exceptions. In life sciences, because you have to go through all the regulations process, so with those we don't expect a return really before the 10-year mark. Unless IPO is in their future, which in the case of one of our most successful companies, Genotobe, they did go with an early IPO, but they are still in the process of going through the regulations.

FP: What factors impact valuation?

NF: Predominantly at this stage it really is down to two-fold, one is revenue. Are they pre- or are they post-revenue, and how much can we bank from their revenue expectations for this year, that they come to us with a Purchase Order for a few hundred thousand dollars and are we more likely to expect valuations to be higher? If, on the other hand, they are coming in pre-revenue, then it's really set by the industry. In general, we follow what the market trends are out there, and we have been in the industry long enough to know what's a realistic valuation expectation and what's not. The second area is really down to that whole market defensibility, simply that they come in with a strong patent portfolio and our experts agree to the fact that these patents are strong and do mean something. Then that will also impact valuation.

FP: Do you often take the position of lead investor?

NF: We are not lead, and it's difficult these days because the company may come to us with a $500K round of which $200K has already been committed. Our investors, I should say our members, actually invest on an individual basis, so we don't actually get involved too much with a single style term sheet. If a company comes to us with a lead, then the terms are usually agreed upon before even coming in. If they don't have a lead, then most of our members have kind of done this enough to know what they want to see in that term sheet. But we are very fair with the companies and we will usually work with the other investors so that to share due-diligence all around and share term sheets whenever possible.

FP: Do you find that people want to take Board seats?

NF: Yes. Board seats are usually a preferred stance for us. It's a great way to make sure that beyond just the capital, we are really offering start-ups the advice that they need, and a good fit has to be there for both entrepreneur and investor. And the real way to protect that is to make sure that we are part of the day-to- day operations of that company, which can really only be secured if we have an advisory or a Board seat position.

FP: Do you find that your Angels tend to invest in companies or industries that they already have previous experience in?

NF: It's desirable that they understand the space they are in, and certainly from the perspective of "they've got contacts that these entrepreneurs would kill for," it makes it very nice. So it's usually a win-win there. Every once in a while a member may see a deal that they understand as a consumer, and choose to invest in the space because they get it from the end perspective. But there definitely has to be a connection on some level, whether it be as a buyer or whether it's just because they know the industry very well.

FP: If you could offer an entrepreneur one piece of advice what would it be?

NF: I think that still the single piece of advice that I would offer to a young start-up is to know when to raise your capital. It's such a full-time position and it requires so much energy and you have to put so many other things on hold while you are fundraising, that it's critical you do it at the right time. Many of our start-ups come to us at too early of a stage to really have much to offer other than just an idea, and an idea that's not fleshed out because they can't dedicate the time to looking into the competitive landscape, to understanding the business model, to knowing what their customers look like and knowing where their exit opportunities lie, that it ends up being a waste of their time, and they become disheartened with the whole side of investing in general. I think that if a company took the time to really work with the customers and the partners, flesh out all of the business in the beginning, and came to us with our ideas already met they would be a lot more successful.

Richard Anders, Managing
Director & Founder

Mass Medical Angels

Boston, MA

www.massmedangels.com

info@massmedicalangels.com

Mass Medical Angels | MA2

FP: This is a new Angel Group, and why did you start it up?

RA: New England is one of the world's hotbeds of life science and healthcare   innovation. While the leading Venture Capital firms have a local presence, we felt the community was lacking a group of sophisticated early-stage life science and healthcare investors which could:

-    help bring new products to the clinic;

-    act as a catalyst for people to engage with other like-minded life science experts for mutual benefit;

-    help in delivering outstanding returns for the primary investors.

FP: How many companies have you invested in so far through the group, and how many do you anticipate you will invest in this year?

RA: We have had three meetings since our first meeting in December 2008. We have closed one investment and have several companies in various stages of diligence. It is premature to speculate about annual throughput at this stage.

FP: How many Angels are part of your group?

RA: We have about 150 people with investing, operating or research experience in   life sciences and healthcare.

FP: How did you personally get interested in Angel investing?

RA: I have been investing for the last 10 years, and earlier had successful experience as an entrepreneur.

FP: What is the average size of investment?

RA: We expect our group to contribute on the order of $100,000-$750,000 for each investment, but we will syndicate with other groups or funds for larger deals.

FP: How do you source deals?

RA: Our members, with considerable experience in life science industry, are a major source of referrals. As we get better known, we get deals through word-of-mouth publicity and from our website.

FP: What is the process for valuating a company?

RA: There is a tremendous depth of experience in our membership, and we rely on their expertise and prior deal making in life science and healthcare markets to decide on what we think is a fair valuation.

FP: What do you look for in an executive summary and what is the most important part of a business plan for you?

RA: In the Executive Summary, we like to read a clear and compelling statement about why this product or service will make a big difference in healthcare.

For the Business Plan, three things are vital: a strong management team; a strong case for how this will be an important innovation in clinical practice (including regulatory approval and reimbursement); and important milestones that our money will allow.

FP: What sort of milestones are you expecting a company to have reached when   they come to you?

RA: We're not looking for a science project. The more validation that has been done, the better chance the company has to secure our investment. The less expensive it is, too, the better. Also, the company should have a strong understanding of their science, regulatory path, clinical adoption potential and possible acquirers.

FP: And how much do the competitive landscape and the size of the market that a company is operating in affect the decision to invest?

RA: A great deal. But we are not interested only in larger markets. For smaller markets that are less competitive, with low financing needs and less risk, we are all ears.

FP: Do you invest in pre-revenue deals?

RA: A better question will be: Do we invest in revenue deals? Yes. Almost all of our deals are pre-revenue.

FP: Do you expect people to come to you with a stated exit strategy?

RA: We really like that.

FP: What do you look for in a management team?

RA: Relevant experience, drive and commitment are important. If the entrepreneur has a strong, successful track record, that is extremely helpful.

FP: Do you require that a company has patents?

RA: It is highly preferred to have patents or other IP protection in place or pending, but they are not always required if being first-to-market can be a huge edge.

FP: What is the general time horizon to a liquidity event, and what are you expecting in terms of ROI?

RA: Our expectations are around 3-7 years for exit, 5x plus returns.

FP: What factors generally impact valuation?

RA: A complete list is too long to state. Here are a few factors (not, by any stretch, all of them):

Experience and formation of the team and Scientific Advisory Board can have a very big positive impact on valuation. The more experienced the entrepreneurs, the better;

The less validation there is, the lower the valuation (up to a point and beyond that, we won't do the deal);

The lower the cash needs for key milestones, the higher the valuation.

FP: Do you ever put together syndicates for investment? Generally, do you take the position of lead investor?

RA: We will syndicate quite happily, and often in Life Science deals this is a necessity. We prefer to lead deals but will certainly follow if another group has brought the deal to us.

FP: If you could offer an entrepreneur only one piece of advice about a seed round and Angels, what would it be?

RA: Find some angels who are willing to mentor you, and work with them for a while. Be willing to show them your business plan, because an overly cautious insistence on confidentiality will make it hard for them to help you. And when you are finally ready to present in front of groups, prepare, prepare, prepare, because you usually get not more than one chance to present to a group, and angel investors are highly networked and look to each other for advice about which companies to consider.

Chris Starr, Managing Director & Vice President of Investments

Innovation Philadelphia & The Mid-Atlantic Angel Group Fund

Philadelphia, Pennsylvania

www.innovationphiladelphia.com & www.magfund.com

info@www.innovationphiladelphia.com & cstarr@sciencecenter.org

215-496-8110

FP: How did you get interested in Angel investing? Can you tell me a little bit more about both Innovation Philadelphia and the Mid-Atlantic Angel Groups.

CS: Sure. Well, I got into the venture capital business about five years ago. And have always been involved in making early-stage investments in technology companies. I have been involved with three different funds. I started out at the Eastern Technology Fund, and that was one of the Safeguard affiliated funds. They were somewhat like CMGI, if you are familiar with them, back in the late '90s. It was a public company that had a variety of venture funds associated with it. After the Eastern Tech Fund I was a principal at Lenfest Capital. And then I was recruited two years ago to come manage the investments for Innovation Philadelphia. Innovation Philadelphia is an earlier-stage company. We do typically seed stage and series A in a wide variety of technology. So we're a generalist fund. And the Mid-Atlantic Angel Group is a second fund that I am a founder of, Mid-Atlantic Angel Group, and we went out and raised 3.3 million and we have approx. 70 individual Angel Investors as part of that, as well as a couple of institutions. It is basically a structured Angel fund. It's a venture capital fund where all of the partners are Angels. And we do, again, seed and series A investments

FP: Do you operate as a fund?

CS: It's a little bit different, basically, in this fund as opposed to a normal venture fund where you've got general partners and then limited partners, and the limited partners, basically, have no say in the investments and the general partners make all the decisions. In the Mid-Atlantic Angel Group fund every member is a partner, and so, I'm the founder and administrator of the fund then. I have facilitated a lot of the dealflow and things like that. Every deal that comes up is voted on by all the members.

FP: Then they have their own option as to whether to invest?

CS: Correct.

FP: You said you looked at a wide variety of industries. Where do you typically invest?

CS: Approximately 40% of our deals are in software, hardware, IT. Approximately 40% is in biotech, pharmaceutical and medical devices. And the remaining 20% is sort of miscellaneous, which would include things like advance materials or services companies or things like that.

FP: How do the deals usually come to you?

CS: We have a quite extensive network through out the mid-Atlantic of relationships with all the service providers including attorneys, accountants, consultants, bankers, investment bankers, and CEOs, and we also have an extensive group of co-investors and folks that we have done deals with before in the venture capital community, so the bulk of our dealflow is referred in.

FP: What's the typical size of an investment?

CS: In the fund that I run for Innovation Philadelphia it's typically $100,000 and the Mid-Atlantic Angel Group is $250,000.

FP: How many companies do you invest in per year?

CS: At Innovation Philadelphia we have 12 companies and we invest in approx. five per year. And the Mid-Atlantic Angel Group fund just closed actually last week, so we haven't made any investment yet but we expect to do two to four per year.

FP: What are your processes for evaluating a company?

CS: They are different in each case.   In the case of Innovation Philadelphia, we solicit the plans or are referred plans; the potential companies fill out online applications that are fairly brief. They submit these applications along with their business plans just in the industries that we are interested in, whether or not they have some sort of critical hurdles that they have to meet given the current funding enviroRAent, and generally whether or not it's worth meeting the company. We will then meet with the company, if we are interested; we will try to get a feel for the management team, and also try to dig in to what we see as the critical issues of the company at that meeting. If, at the end of that meeting, we are still interested, we will begin due-diligence, and that involves all the usual aspects of research and the market, competitors, the product, the team, legal background, financials and so on. Depending on what issues are found, that process can take as little as six weeks all the way up to typically lasting to six months. During this time there will normally be several more meetings with the company, and during that time while conducting due-diligence, at which point we bring it to an investment committee and our investment committee makes the final decision whether or not we invest in the company.

Now, the Mid-Atlantic Angel Group process is somewhat similar except that after the deals are screened we select three deals per month to present to the group and we require 50% vote from the group to move a company forward to due-diligence. And once we have completed that due-diligence, which is preformed by a member of the group, another vote is taken which requires a 67% vote of all the members to move a company into getting the deal done.

FP: What do you look for in a business plan?

CS: We pretty much look for most of the same things that most venture groups do. We are looking for, first and foremost, a good business opportunity, some compelling business case. The second thing we look for is a management team that's able to execute that business. The third thing, an attractive and growing market that is not saturated already. We look for competitive differentiation, something that makes this company unique and sustainable. We look for technology that is protectable, whether it is through legal means or competitive means. We look for companies that can grow 50 to $100 million in revenue in a five-to seven-year period. We look for companies that have some reasonable prospect of achieving an exit.

FP: What do you look for in terms of a return on investment?

CS: We look for returns of approx. 10 times our initial investment.

FP: Are you generally looking for a stated exit strategy?

CS: Not so much a stated exit strategy, but we are looking for companies that would be reasonably exitable, meaning that there may be multiple opportunities for exit, whether through acquisition, if it's an acquisition strategy, that there might be, you know, five to 10 potential buyers that would be interested. We are less interested in something that may only have one buyer. We typically look for something that might have multiple possible exits, acquisition and possible IPO. The more the better.

FP: What sort of milestones are you looking for the company to have achieved, particularly if it is pre-revenue?

CS: Well, there is a wide difference between the regular portfolio and the biotech portion of the portfolio. Right now we see very few companies that are getting funded that are in the pre-revenue stage. I should clarify that by saying we are seeing very few companies receiving institutional funding at the pre-revenue stage, and that may be unique to our market but that's what we are seeing. That does not hold, obviously, for biotech. Biotech is a unique animal and, you know, we see plenty of appetite for companies that are obviously - they are all pre-revenue, we are seeing appetite for companies that are just about to be in or are already in their phase one clinicals.

FP: What do you look for in a management team?

CS: One of the biggest things that we factor in is the quality in the management team. Given the dealflow that we have, we are fortunate to be able to select fairly mature, experienced management teams. So just about all of our CEOs have already achieved an exit in another company. They have either taken something public or sold it. Several of them have done that several times. So this tends to be a fairly mature, experienced group. We tend not to fund young first- time CEOs. We have a couple of them, but they are fairly well-experienced people. Otherwise we just don't have that much interest in backing them because there is enough good opportunity with good creditable management teams out there right now.

FP: What do you consider when you are evaluating a company?

CS: Right now most of the companies that we are investing in have valuations pre-money of one to three million. We try to take a preferred look at companies that are sub five million pre-money. If things are valued well beyond that we typically won't even look at them, and the reason for that is because if the valuation is too high at this early stage, we are taking on too much risk, and the possibility for return generally isn't large enough for us to get the multiples we are looking for.

FP: Now, do you often put together syndicates for investments and do you take the lead investor position?

CS: We typically are a part of a syndicate.

FP: If you could offer an entrepreneur only one piece of advice regarding a seed round and Angels, what would it be?

CS: First of all, I don't know if I would be capable of only giving one piece of advice, but I think the key for me would be for them to raise enough money to get to a funding milestone, whatever that might be for the company. So they have to be careful not to raise too little money and run out of it... enough money that it can get them to the point in development of the company that another round of capital would be able to be raised to continue scaling the company. That might be a revenue target, it might be a number of customers, it might be a certain product development, it might be a regulatory hurdle that needs to be passed, and it might be setting up a production facility, whatever that might be for that company. Typically, it is revenue. It is either hitting some revenue number or some hurdle that will suddenly make the company interesting to a wide variety of funding sources. For example, if we fund a company that is doing $1 million in revenue we know that it's probably going to need to get to $4 million to $5 million in revenue before the larger institutional VCs are going to have much interest. That is just an example but ... in a case of many software companies, until they get to that level, most of the larger institutional VCs aren't going to have much interest, and that will be one of the top priorities, raising enough money that the company can scale to that level and to the next round.

NOTE: the new executive director of the MAG Fund is Karen Griffith Gryga

Dee Harris, President

Arizona Angels

2415 E. Camelback Road,
Suite 700, Phoenix, AZ
85016

www.arizonaangels.com

info@arizona-angels.org

ARIZONANGELS

FP: This is a new Angel Group, and why did you start it up?

DH: The Arizona Angels was organized in 1999. It was the first angel group in Arizona. The founders believed that there was insufficient capital in Arizona available to start-up and young companies. This problem was exacerbated by the presence in the State of relatively few venture capital firms.

FP: How many companies have you invested in so far through the group, and how many do you anticipate you will invest in this year?

DH: Since formation, the Angels have invested in approximately twenty to twenty-five companies. Because of the recession, we probably will not invest in more than two or three in 2009.

FP: How many Angels are in your group currently?

DH: Approximately 30 investors attend any given meeting—not always the same people.

FP: How did you personally get interested in Angel investing?

DH: I have always been interested in capital formation. I majored in economics as an undergraduate and then became a securities lawyer. More recently, I observed the link between innovation and capital, and how an area with a large number of entrepreneurial companies has a healthier and more diversified economy.

FP: What is the average size of investment?

DH: Our investments in a single company have ranged from $100,000 to $540,000. Increasingly, we are collaborating with other angel groups in the region in an attempt to raise larger sums for companies whose capital needs exceed those amounts.

FP: How do you source deals?

DH: Most deals come to us via Internet—usually by Angelsoft applications to our website. However, our advisory board and selection committee members are also actively seeking to discover promising companies.

FP: What is the process for valuating a company?

DH: I review the application, which almost always includes an executive summary or a full business plan. I send electronically the most promising applications to the selection committee. The committee members rate the applications using the Angelsoft software and indicate whether they wish to see the CEO of the applicant present at a committee meeting. Normally, four companies are chosen to make a PowerPoint presentation to the committee. The presentations are followed by Q&A. Two or three companies are chosen to present to the full membership later. Sometimes the company will seem promising, but the CEO has not put together a compelling presentation, in which case, we will arrange for one or a few people to help polish the presentation before it is delivered.

FP: What do you look for in an executive summary and what is the most important part of a business plan for you?

DH: While many things are very important, the single-most essential element is a qualified management team. Almost equally important is the potential for the company to grow its revenues rapidly so that the fifth-year-after-funding revenues are projected to be at least $20 million.

FP: What sort of milestones are you expecting a company to have reached when they come to you?

DH: We do not require applicants to have revenues, but they must demonstrate traction in some way, which might include patents obtained or applied for, promising conversations with large customers, or manufacturing arrangements made.

FP: And how much do the competitive landscape and the size of the market that a company is operating in affect the decision to invest?

DH: The competitive landscape and the size of the market are very important.

FP: Do you invest in pre-revenue deals?

DH: We do invest in pre-revenue companies.

FP: Do you expect people to come to you with a stated exit strategy?

DH: It helps if the entrepreneur has thought deeply about an exit strategy. If they don't mention likely acquirers in their presentations, the members will ask. Most convincing are entrepreneurs who have formed a judgment about which specific companies or classes of companies are likely to be natural acquirers. Since even in good years very few companies are able to go public, we discount statements about possible IPOs. Arrangements to buy the investors' position with profits from the company are also disfavored.

FP: What do you look for in a management team?

DH: Management teams should be at least two or three persons with diverse qualifications. The entrepreneur needs to already understand that over time, and with funding, the management team will need to grow and to have thought about what roles the new team members will fill. Relatives on management teams are strongly discouraged. A one-person management team is always rejected.

FP: Do you require that a company has patents?

DH: We look for a sustainable competitive advantage whenever possible. Patents or patents pending are very desirable, but are not the only way of obtaining such a competitive advantage. We realize that many companies are doing something that cannot be patented.

FP: What is the general time horizon to a liquidity event, and what are you expecting in terms of ROI?

DH: We expect an exit in three to five years. Because many companies fail outright or do not meet their original goals, we look for the remaining investments to do very well and to generate an overall return for the portfolio. In this regard, we are like professional venture capitalists. We do not have a particular required ROI, but it is hoped that each company has the potential to return invested capital several fold.

FP: What factors generally impact valuation?

DH: Valuation is determined by whether the company has revenue, the quality of the management team, the sustainable competitive advantage, the competitive landscape, the amount of prior investment, the size of the market, the elegance and uniqueness of the business model, and the projected future revenues.

FP: Tell me a little bit about term sheets. How do you go in there?

DH: After a company makes a presentation to the full membership, those members who are interested will follow up with the CEO, usually as a group. If they determine to invest, they will negotiate a term sheet with the entrepreneur.

FP: Do you ever put together syndicates for investment? Generally, do you take the position of lead investor?

DH: We have jointly invested with the Desert Angels in Tucson, we have considered a Vegas Valley Angels deal, and we are seeking to collaborate with the New Mexico Angels. Usually, the lead is the first group to decide to go forward.

FP: If you could offer an entrepreneur only one piece of advice about a seed round and Angels, what would it be?

DH: Arrogance, cockiness, and stubbornness are fatal to an entrepreneur's chances of obtaining funding from knowledgeable strangers. Investors are looking for entrepreneurs who are willing to listen and to change course when necessary. We use the term "coachable" to refer to this trait. If the primary entrepreneur and prospective is a technologist without prior business experience, or is otherwise not likely to be proficient at managing the company when it starts to grow rapidly, we ask if he or she is willing to move into some other management role (perhaps Chief Technology Officer or Chief Science Officer) if necessary. From our perspective, the correct answer to that question is: "Yes, I would absolutely be willing to do so if it would help the company succeed."

Chris Saxman

New York Angels

New York, New York

www.newyorkangels.com

info@newyorkangels.com

212-459-7388

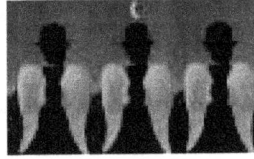

FP: How did you get interested in Angel investing, and what is the background of the New York Angels?

CS: A friend of mine, who was a Venture Capitalist, suggested that I talk to the people at NYRAA (New York New Media Association). NYRAA had an Angel investing group which turned into the New York Angels group subsequently, but it was sort of run like an event planning thing. When these guys did it, they just sort of went out and found some people with money, some people who wanted more money, people who wanted to invest, to put these two together. And that was much to the extent of what they did. So there was - it was hard to get the momentum around having one of these deals done. So, I came in and my idea was I would help them provide a little more structure and investment rigor and they could, in terms of the long run, kind of use it as a platform to look. So, that's kind of what we did. And then New York Angels, the way the New York Angels started is in the end of 2003, NYRAA was shut down and the group, the Angel Investors were flourishing and they didn't want to sort of shut down and expand, so they decided to set up an independent group – that's kind of what we did.

FP: Are you a fund?

CS: No, we are not a fund. We - actually we do work as if we were a fund, up to the point where a decision needs to be made. Then, each individual investor will make his or her own decision as to whether they go into something or not. So, no, we are not a fund.

FP: Are there specific industries in which the group invests?

CS: We won't look at biotech or nanotech, things that involve really heavy science just because we don't feel as though we have the expertise to do that. What we do look at, I'd say the bulk of what we look at is IT, or IT-related, but we've been looking at some non-tech companies and products recently, as well.

FP: How many companies have you invested in?

CS: In 2004, we invested in eight; we invested in five in 2003, actually, six, I guess. Maybe we'll get more when we have better deal stores and more Angels.

FP: What's the average size of investment?

CS: $250K to $750K.

FP: How do you source deals?

CS: A lot of them come in through Angels, the network of individual Angels – so somebody will come in and just ask, instead of looking at it individually he will bring it in to us. Another source is through Venture Capitalists, who see deals that are too early stage – they are looking for money, so we'll do that. Where else? We get them from things like your group and we get them from - well, we're beginning to work with incubators and other things like that.

FP: What is the process for valuating the company?

CS: Well, we've got a bit of a process; we've got a fairly good, rigorous screening process. When the company first comes to us, I'll take a first look at it and if I like it, then I'll invite the company to come to a screening meeting in which I invite two or three or four Angels and we listen to the pitch. We hear probably 10 or 12 a month in this form, and then we select three or four companies to go to a larger meeting where they can pitch to the entire group.

FP: How many Angels are in the group?

CS: We currently have 48. So then it goes to the whole group. If individuals are interested, we'll sit with them, sort of a two-hour-long meeting with the company and after that, if they are still interested, after we've fully sort of checked them out a little bit, then we will start doing real due-diligence. We start going through a due-diligence list that we sort of use. We go through the term sheet, put together a deal.

FP: How long is due-diligence? How long is the screening to the final meeting and then if it passes "GO," how long is the next part?

CS: Screening generally happens in the middle of the month, the final meeting is at the end of the month – we do it every month. Diligence... the first sit-down meeting is the week afterwards and then it could take anywhere from 30 to... well, I would say anywhere from 60 to a hundred and eighty days to close the deal. Doing the diligence, you can get that done – some of these deals we've moved quicker in terms of due-diligence but typically, we'd say four to six weeks to complete diligence on the deal. And then after that it's going to be negotiating, and the time involved in negotiating is going to be the deal and the final documents.

FP: What do you look for in an executive summary and what is the most important part of a business plan for you?

CS: Well, I would say the most important part of a business plan is - well, there are sort of two things. One is the quality of the team; everyone says that one, but it's true. Two is the realism, the realistic – the second one is my evaluation, or my evaluation of how realistic the opportunity and how realistic is it that the company is going to be able to exploit that opportunity. So, the author of the plan needs discipline to clearly articulate what it is that he has, what he sells, why that is valuable – why there is value in what he sells. The best way to do that is to demonstrate why his customers **need** the product, as opposed to why his customers might find the product kind of fun or interesting. If you can show demonstrated need for a particular product, that's what we want. Then, thirdly, you have to show why it is that he is going to be able to deliver his product without competition.

Initially, we look at the executive summary and we have a one-page summary that goes with the executive summary that we ask people to fill out which has - it basically asks them to list every key area and aspect of their business. Initially, we take a very high view and that's why the author of these things has to be able to write clearly.

FP: What sort of milestones are you expecting a company to have reached when they come to you?

CS: Generally, we look for companies to have finished product development. We expect them to be ready to begin selling their product, or better yet, that they have already begun to fill their product mass.

FP: Do you invest in pre-revenue deals?

CS: Yes. But typically, the ones that we're most interested in are not the pre-revenue. You know, post-revenue.

FP: When you're looking at an investment, do you expect the market that the company is operating in to be a certain size?

CS: I don't so much care about the size of the market. I mean, how do you measure the size of a market in three years? Anyone can tell you what <the size of the market is> going to be... I don't know how those estimates are put together, right? What I would be much more interested in knowing is what the company's own revenue projections are going to be. I want to know that it has the potential to grow into at least a 50 million dollar revenue company in five years, say. I don't necessarily want them to show me how they'll reach 50 million dollars in their projections, I just need to know that this is a company that has the potential to grow progressively early on and build substantial revenues - enough that would attract somebody to buy them. What I'm really concerned with is exit. I want to know how I'm going to get out. What I don't want to do is invest in lifestyle businesses, you know, run it up to five million dollars in revenue and just kind of stay there, or generate three or four hundred thousand dollars each year. Their dividends are paid but that's not what I want. I want a business that's going to grow very rapidly.

The reason why I am uncomfortable with saying that "I want a billion dollar market" is these guys are going to get five percent of this, and that's sort of a top-down analysis, and I don't like companies that do this. I want a bottom-up analysis. I don't want you to say, "Here are the top 10 customers in my industry that I'm going to go after. The number four customer I've got a letter of intent with and he tells me he's going to buy x number of dollars from me, and number six customer we've actually signed a contract with, and the number one customer we're in discussions with, and I estimate that he'll buy x from me. And when I add all of this up, this is my pipeline and what I think I can get over the next three years." See, I can understand that. Starting from the customers. What you are going to do?

FP: What do you look for in a management team?

CS: Clearly, if a manager has successfully run an entrepreneurial business before and sold it, I think that's impressive. I look for people that have some grab with us. In other words, who present themselves, who have a certain, I don't know, the feeling of being seasoned. In other words, a business-like professional. As you begin to discuss and you begin to talk to people and probe into difficult subjects and areas where a person just might not be well filled out, the way that they handle that kind of adversity tells me a lot about the maturity of the person, if you know what I mean. It's not always evident at first glance, but I can think of several people who have recently, where they, at first, seemed very confident, they have done some interesting things, but they just didn't seem to have all of the answers. I look for management, I want to look further down the management team. I want people who have had experience in whatever the current business is.

FP: How fleshed out does the management team need to be?

CS: Obviously, they need to have a CEO, I need to know who the VP is, where the technology came from, if it's a technology company, I'd like to talk to the technologist. I want to know that, if that's key, I want to know that there's a good technologist on board. A lot of the businesses we deal in aren't necessarily technology businesses, or not ones where there is hard-core technology needed. In those cases, it might be sales and marketing that is key. So, I want to know who the marketing person is. I guess, what I want to have in place, is whoever the key people for running that sort of business is. We're looking at a company who is going to sell things by walking into Wal-Mart, so for them, they are going to need a great marketer, but they are also going to need a great finance guy. If you're going to have to deal with inventory and managing working capital, you have to manage carefully. So, in that team, you usually want to know who the CFO is. Other places the CFOs aren't that important.

FP: So, do you expect people to come to you with a stated exit strategy?

CS: Well, I think that the answer to that is almost every exit strategy for the companies we invest in is going to be – selling to a strategic buyer. In general, our company isn't going to go IPO – in general. So, they are going to sell out, okay, great. I guess what I want to know is, not so much what their exit strategy is going to be, because I know what it's going to be, I want to know that they are, indeed, planning to exit. Under what conditions, sort of when, that their management team wants to get out of there as badly as I do.

FP: What's the general time horizon to a liquidity event, and what are you expecting in terms of ROI?

CS: We're investing pretty early so the time horizon could be anywhere in the five- to seven-year range. I think that we hope to make at least 10 times our money in a deal, maybe more than that, maybe 20 times our money because it's early in the deal. So that's basically what we're looking for, in general. We don't do a whole hell of a lot of our financial modeling in terms of prediction and that sort of thing, we just sort of - again, we just want to know that if we invest in a company that is pre-revenue or maybe has 100,000 in revenue, that we expect that it can get to 50 million in revenue, then we're going to make a hell of a lot of money because with a new company, we typically invest in valuations in the one- to three-million dollar range. We've done a couple of deals at four million dollars, but typically, that's where the companies at our stage should be unless there's some truly astounding thing of value. Like a patent that's pretty iron clad that gives the company a walk in the market. That is pretty clearly valuable. That is something we pay up for. In general, most of the companies we pay for are not that sexy that they would warrant above a five million dollar pre-revenue valuation at the level we look at. Although certainly we come across companies who think they are.

FP: What factors generally impact valuation?

CS: Quality of management team, stage of investing, stage of company – how close they are to revenue positive, what customers they have.

If we were looking at some real funding option models – that might be relevant to look at, but no, it's just basically, similar to valuing real estate, it's like, where did the last transaction trade? It's all comparative. Not models, mind you. Just looking at similar transactions. Having a feel for the market and how things trade. Also, knowing what our return expectations are. Again, if you want 10 to 20 or 30 times your money and the company is going to sell in four years, and in four years they expect to have 25 million dollars and you go in with a two million dollar pre- and you expect that they are going to trade at two times their money, at 25 million dollars, they'd sell at 50 million dollars. Well, then you've made 25 times your money, which is good, it's about right. So, it's not really a whole lot more sophisticated than that. But by the same token, a lot of these companies, if we go in much more than, if we went in five or six million pre-revenue, then it would be harder, they would have to sell for a lot more. I guess another issue that we have to be concerned about is how much additional capital they are going to need because, we can't always continue to fund the company. We don't want to be crammed down by the Venture Capitalist, which is actually a real risk in a lot of these companies. So, we have to, in a way that we can protect ourselves, go in at a low valuation.

FP: Tell me a little bit about term sheets. How do you go in there?

CS: We have a standard convertible note we use and we have a standard series A preferred that we use. Pretty plain vanilla things.

FP: What would cause you to take a convertible note over equity?

CS: That's a good question. The advantage over a convertible note is that they are, well, they're a note so there's a downside that you could stand above the other creditors for sort of liquidation. You also avoid setting a price. Typically we do convertible notes with a collar. We go in on some discounts on future rounds, up to a certain point. But that on that side, it is that it's easier for the next round to cram you down. If you've actually come in and set up a valuation, then you know what that valuation is going to be, but if you let the other guy set up the valuation, then you don't know what it's going to be and you might get screwed.

FP: Do you ever put together syndicates for investment? Generally, do you take the position of lead investor?

CS: Sure. It depends; if we were going into a Venture Capitalist round then obviously the VC would be competing. If it's an Angel syndicate, we generally do like to lead, but there are other Angel Groups that lead, as well. We're looking at one right now, Jumpstart New Jersey, we're leading the negotiations and the term sheets but we're sharing the diligence with them.

FP: If you could offer an entrepreneur only one piece of advice about a seed round and Angels, what would it be?

CS: A key piece of advice, a key thing they need to know... I think that the key piece of advice is, from my point of view, to have a very realistic understanding of why their business is going to make money. Why their business can be profitable and can be well profitable. To understand that, when I say, "realistic," I mean understand the logic of what it is you are saying and be sure that logic is sound. That incorporates a lot of things. It encompasses figuring out what the competition is, why you're better than the competition, understanding why your strategy is sound, understanding if there is a real need for the product, if there's a real need, and defining the product and market appropriately. Make sure you are targeting towards the appropriate market, the equity story holds true.

NOTE: Chris Saxman is the former Executive Director of the NY Angels. The Current Executive Director is Paul Sciabica

Lou Anne Flanders-Stec,
Fund Executive
Piedmont Angel Network
Greensboro, North Carolina
www.piedmontangelnetwork.com
lafstec@piedmontangelnetwork.com
336-235-0941

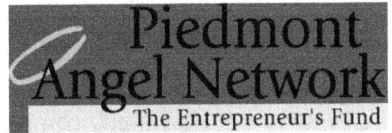

Piedmont Angel Network
The Entrepreneur's Fund

FP: Tell me a little bit about the background of the Piedmont Angel Network (PAN).

LF: Okay. The group was formed officially with their first close in December of 2001. They began the process in mid 2000 with the Small Business Technology Development Center, Piedmont Entrepreneurs Network and a couple of very interested Angel Investor individuals. What they saw in our region was, as everyone else does, a capital gap. They decided to fill that gap. We had four leaders, from our four major cities/regions who lead the process in the Triad region, which is a 12-county region.

FP: Okay, so you've got representatives from which four cities?

LF: From Greensboro, High Point, Winston-Salem, and then there's a little bit of a northern eastern region which starts at Burlington and spreads all the way over to Mount Airy, which is north on the way to Virginia. So those are the four regions that we really tried to pool our investors in. So, those four leaders pooled together their Rolodex and started making their phone calls. Like I said, they had their first close in December of '01 with two and a quarter million dollars and began running the fund. It was officially administered by the Piedmont Entrepreneurs Network, or PEN, and they hired me in April of '02. They made their first two investment decisions in March of '02 and closed those later on in the '02 year. We left the fund open for new investors until February of '04 when we closed it out with almost four and a half million in total fund amount with 81 members. We are a fund rather than a group that does individual investments. Our individual members can invest in what we call an add-on, and so that's where we head. Our goal is to do 10 investments from this fund, so that would mean that you would do about $400,000 in each investment from the fund. We range from $200K-$300K in the first round depending on the industry the company is in. If it's a biotech company we start on the low end so we have lots of dry powder. And our investments to date in the first round have ranged from $200,000 to almost $700,000 with add-ons.

FP: How many companies have you invested in?

LF: We've closed eight, we're working to close the ninth now, and so we are looking for our tenth. In that process, so that we don't skip a beat, we are looking at our second fund, which we hope to close some time in February '05.

FP: Will the second fund be comparable in size?

LF: That is our goal. Our goal actually is to have it bigger, but right now we're going to have our first close with 50 members and two and a half million minimum.

FP: So, how many deals do you do a year?

LF: We did two deals in '02, we did four deals in '03 and voted on three deals in '04, with one closing in '05.

FP: Are there specific industries in which you invest?

LF: We've really taken a diversified portfolio attitude both in industry and in stage. We have one portfolio company that we invested in their 11 million dollar B round. That was a strategic decision, it was a later stage-deal, even though the technology was still pretty early stage, with one of the VCs in our state, to partner with them and to just really be a part of a bigger group. Now, we've probably rethought that a little bit and I don't know if we'll do that again in PAN 2, the reason being that we really, really like to have the impact on the company. With our investment amount, they don't ignore us, but we don't have the impact like we do with the company that we're trying to close now where we are the only investor. That's why people do Angel investing.

FP: Have you had any deals that are very specifically regional? I mean all of your deals are local to a certain extent.

LF: All of our deals are all within a three-hour drive, and we have five that are in the Triad, four that are out, or it may be - yes, four that are out of the Triad. One in Southern Virginia, two in Raleigh, and one in Charlotte. There are a couple that we're very excited about regionally, but one in particular is a gentleman that has 42 patents to his name that has moved to this region from Atlanta to take advantage of the Piedmont Triad Research Park facilities. Now he has partnered with one of our serial entrepreneurs in our region, so it's working very, very well. He's not having to divert his attention from development to spend so much time or money on FDA approval process. This company has the approval processes in place and I think have completed 12 or 13 medical devices through the FDA approval. He's got a device patent, they've got contacts nationwide and internationally, and manufacturing and FDA capabilities, and it's really ramped him up so much quicker. I really don't think that would've happened if he stayed in Atlanta. So he's thrilled, we're thrilled and it's working really well. We closed that investment in July and things were already moving quickly for them.

FP: What is the process by which you evaluate a company?

LF: We have a couple of passes; the first pass is through me. I will do an executive summary overview, and if there are questions that I think a business plan will answer, I'll ask for a business plan. I will then spend, if it's a company that I feel the members would be interested in, 45 minutes to an hour on a phone call. If it's a company that I think that the members would be interested in that's not ready, then I will put the company in touch with a multitude of other resources. And at times, I'll take them under my wing and help them myself. I just don't have the time to do that on a regular basis. So, that process is anywhere, depending on dealflow, from two weeks to three months. At this point, we have so much dealflow people are having to wait two months before they go to the next step. Then you go through the screening meeting, and we have a screening committee of nine that meets once a month to see three to four companies, and they, at that point in time, do their pitch. They have 15 to 18 minutes to pitch and then we do Q&A for about 30 minutes in total per company. We're trying to figure out a way to extend that time because we really feel like it's very valuable time. At that point, it takes a unanimous vote of those who are officially on the screening committee to move the company to the membership, which can sometimes get interesting. We've got a little bartering that goes on every once in awhile: "I like that one but you don't, you like another one, but I don't. I'll swap you!" It has really worked well. If you're a member of PAN but not a member of the screening committee, it just takes the majority of those members. So, that is step two. If they go to the membership, that would be step three. They have an even shorter time for presentation to allow a longer time for questions. We give them only 12 minutes for presentation and we end up with 20 to 25 minutes for the questions. And at that point in time we do a secret ballot vote for due-diligence. It takes a simple majority to go to due- diligence.

FP: Out of that group of Angels, do people sort of self-nominate to do due-diligence?

LF: Exactly. But, one of the things that we've really tried to do is not have an entrepreneur walk away with just a "no". They will always walk away with a "no" and here's the reason why. They get, usually, four to five very specific things that are issues to our group that may be very specific to us, and my goal is to make sure they understand why we said no and why we think that other groups may say yes just because we're all in different places.

FP: Since you are seeing executive summaries and business plans all of the time, what makes a good executive summary and/or business plan?

LF: The executive summary needs to tell me there's a problem, tell me how they are going to solve it, tell me that the market is big enough to make a difference from an investment standpoint, and that the people that are there doing it have either done it before or have such a background in the industry that they know where to go or who to talk to, to get it accomplished. Those are really the things that I look for. It doesn't have to be a paradigm shift, because sometimes the simplest things are the most successful. That's really what I need to see, and basic financials. When you get to the business plan, I want them to be defining what the market is, the relevant market, their sales strategy, marketing plans, a little more detail on financials and their exit strategy and who they know would be an acquiring party.

FP: Do you invest in pre-revenue deals?

LF: Yes.

FP: What sort of milestones, either from pre-revenue deals or from later stage which you said you did, as well, are you looking for the company to have accomplished before investment?

LF: Really, we don't like pre-prototype deals. So we want them to have a prototype. We want them to have an addressable way to reach their relevant market. We want, oftentimes, an advisory board of people that they can pull from and tap, and usually the expanse of the management team to already be determined. Not that they've hired them, but that at least they know who they need and who they want.

FP: What do you look for in a company's management team?

LF: Truly, truly, experience. It's both from "has been there done that" experience in an early-stage company as well as relevant industry experience.

FP: You mentioned the size of the market that the company is going to be working in. Do you have a minimum in terms of what this market size will be?

LF: It really depends on product scope, add-on products, and things like that. I would say that if a market is under 200 million our group is probably not going to consider it, even remotely. The reason, you just have to go back and do the numbers related to desired return.

FP: In terms of intellectual property, do you require that companies have patents or what kind of IP protection?

LF: No, we don't require the company to have patents. If it is a patentable product or item, we have an intellectual property attorney that can be the coach. He has advised a multitude of times both for PAN and for the company on some strategy, and that is one of our big value-adds. He is not of the opinion that everything needs to be patented, so he's been very, very helpful in that arena. Now, there's a company that we're looking at now that has trade secrets and some additional know-how surrounding their technology and he's very, very comfortable that they don't go the patent route because it's a very, very unique process. So those are the kinds of things that we kind of look through to the reality of the situation instead of just saying, "You've got to have a patent."

FP: What do you expect the time horizon to be to a liquidity event?

LF: Oh, boy. Crystal ball. I will tell you that we have two companies that already had intended to exit at this point. The market changes so quickly and the situations change so quickly. The whole landscape has changed. It changes within a matter of months. We would've loved to have had an exit before we started a second fund. That recruitment effort would've been very easy. But, looking at our portfolio, we've got a couple of decent opportunities for the five- year exits. So, 2006, '07, '08 timeframe is what I would hope for, but again, who knows!

FP: Do you expect companies to come with a stated exit strategy?

LF: Very much so. That's one of the things that I battle with the most from an entrepreneurial standpoint, unrealistic valuations and the fact that they don't really need to be focusing on an exit strategy. If you don't have one in mind from day one, it's going to become a second thought and then a third thought and then a fourth thought, and we really want the company to have a goal of an exit.

FP: What, in general, is the expectation in terms of ROI?

LF: We talk less about ROI and talk more about time earnings. If a company does not have the capacity to do a 10X return in three years, four years, with their stated revenue discounted, then we're not going to look at them. Our goal for the fund would probably be realistically, if we did 3X over the life of the fund, we'd be very pleased. That would probably translate to about a 30% ROI, I think.

FP: What factors impact the valuation?

LF: Let's see. All of the factors we've talked about. Management, IP, market, process. If it's pre-prototype or just prototype and there's no testing done, we focus largely on competition. We also like to see what else is going on in the market. Often a company comes in and says, "I've got zero revenue but I've got a great market and I want to do a six million dollar valuation." You then just have to honestly say, "I know we aren't talking about the same industry, but I've got companies that are coming to me looking for money that have revenue, even if just 500,000 that are doing expansion rounds at two and a half to three million in valuation". So, it's - really, it's a numbers game. The return calculation or back end of the numbers game that the members really put their hands around. Now, we will do a high valuation, trust me. We've done two because we certainly believed in the company so, so much.

FP: Do you often put syndicates together for investments, and are you always the lead investor?

LF: We have led two of the nine. We have put together one syndicate. We didn't put it together actually, one of the other Angel Networks in North Carolina put it together. And we co-invest often on deals that are already in place or in process.

FP: We talked a little bit about due-diligence. How long does that process generally take?

LF: Too long! There are two factors, but first and foremost the time starts ticking as soon as I send the due-diligence checklist to the company. Often they will forget the time it took for them to send us the materials and then get frustrated because the process takes so long. So, the due-diligence process we're in now on one company, it took six weeks to get the due-diligence materials. So, that one is going to take four months. The one that we are working on now, the new one we just voted on, will probably take two months. In normal days, if we get the due-diligence materials within a reasonable time frame, it's 60 to 75 days.

FP: What is your background?

LF: My background is all over the board, from family business to half-way through my MBA, taking a position as a financial analyst for a poultry manufacturer. I worked my way up to Director of Budget & Planning for the sales department. That's really where I probably stepped away from more of an analyst role to a big picture role. From there, I ended up again in manufacturing, with a hat manufacturer, as their cash and treasury director and working with the banks. We were highly, highly levered, so that was an eye-opening experience. Eventually, I worked with a group setting up a small venture fund as their CFO. Did a couple of deals there, moved to North Carolina, worked for an Internet start-up in the bubble as their CFO. Raised a million and a half dollars in about eight to 10 weeks, and then went out for a second round in August of 2000. We lasted until February of '01. After a time as CFO for our local United Way, I transitioned to PAN because I really wanted to get back into the venture, finance arena.

FP: Now, do you participate in this group as an Angel?

LF: Yes, I do.

FP: What do you like most about Angel investing?

LF: I think that... it brings all my experiences together. The experience with the venture fund, including legal documents – the deal terms – and also the big picture in the manufacturing world, but especially that of being the CFO for a start-up. I was knocking on the doors of all of the people that I'm doing deals with now. Like the Charlotte Angel Partners, I stood in front of their group as the CFO and asked for money. So, I know exactly what entrepreneurs as well as investors are going through. It's great to watch a company grow, be a part of that growth, and help build value and a return for our investors and the management team.

FP: You mentioned doing the legal documents. What do term sheets look like?

LF: We prefer to do preferred series A or B. We have done a couple of convertible notes but that was on a very short-term basis. We knew that the round was coming or it was between the first and second round, and that's really when we've done the convertible notes.

FP: Once you've put money into a deal, what do you expect to be the next set of milestones for the company?

LF: Again, it depends on where the company is. We've got a couple of companies that we've put milestones in. One of them, there's some software development that they've got tagged and some products that they are going to be offering through that software, and those are the milestones.

We've got another company that we've got some sales milestones because they've started the revenue track. So it just really depends on the industry, and what the product is, and where they are in the process.

FP: If you could offer an entrepreneur only one piece of advice regarding seed rounds and Angel Investors, what would it be?

LF: Be "coach-able," and in that "coach-ability" you've got to build realism – be realistic. Get at least one advisor around you, preferably multiple, who have done it before and that you can call day or night.

FP: That notion of the advisor or the champion has come across again and again in the interview. It has really been fascinating.

LF: You know, you say it and you say it and you say it and they still don't get it. That's why I keep saying it, because it really does help. The people you talk to that found advisors will tell you the same thing. I recently sat on a panel with a couple who built a business and they told everyone the best thing they ever did was make a phone call to SCORE, which is one of our entrepreneurial organizations, who assigned them an advisor that guided them and helped them fix many of their problems, as well as prepared them for the pitfalls of a new business. So, anybody that goes out and does it will tell you the same thing, but for some reason, entrepreneurs don't hear that.

Tom Grant

The Richmond Venture Forum

Richmond, Virginia

www.ventureclub.com

tom.grant@troutmansanders.com

804-267-3370

FP: Tell us a little bit more about the Richmond Venture Forum and how you got involved in Angel investing.

TG: The Richmond Venture Forum was probably founded about 20 years ago, and at that time it was focused solely on introducing Angels to entrepreneurs. As the economy changed, waned and waxed, Angel investors declined, we found ourselves in July of 2004 with a new board of which I am the president. Figuring what's the mission of the institution, we reckoned that we needed to change the mission into basically three components. One is education, two is networking and three is creating an Angel database, with the override of all of those being that we identified our target market as being emerging growth companies, not lifestyle companies, meaning people that just want to kind of run the business for their own family purposes, not really become expansive. But we decided that of the emerging company marketplace we broke that down into an early-stage, mid-stage and latter-stage. Basically, early-stage is from no revenues up to a million bucks, mid-stage is one million to 15 million, and latter-stage is 15 million probably to 50 million. And what we decided is that we would concentrate of that group in the mid-stage emerging company arena.

So all of our programs really are aimed at helping those people. And we also are trying to tie in the local resources, small business development centers, that are trying to help the early-stage so we don't want to be predominantly in that business. But we want to take the latter-stage companies who have achieved some semblance of success and get the management of those companies to work with the mid-stage and early-stage companies, to give back to the community. So the programs involve them.

And then, what you could probably guess, <we are> supported by the lawyers, the accountants, the investment bankers, I mean those are the guys that really fund the organization, although we want to get the entrepreneurs funded. So we are making everything aimed at networking, so the service providers can get access to potential clients.

The last arm is the hardest arm, and that is to work towards creating pretty much an active Angel database here in Richmond, which we have temporarily tabled while all these other re-organizational efforts are going on. But that will probably come back to critical development I'd say, May or June of this year.   And the background of that idea, essentially, is to create a confidential database that entrepreneurs can send messages through to registered Angels, and if any of them are interested they can contact the entrepreneurs at that time. It would be sort of a non-identifiable base from the Angels' point of view, unless they want to signal their identities to specific entrepreneurs.

FP: Now do you personally invest as an Angel?

TG: Yeah, yeah, I do.

FP: But there is no fund that has been created by the Angels in your group?

TG: No, not in Richmond, Virginia.

FP: What attracted you to Angel investing?

TG: Well, two things. One is, I think some part of my portfolio ought to be pretty speculative. And two is because of the business I'm in as an attorney here, it is one of those attractions for clients that are entrepreneurs to know that either I can be willing to consider an investment myself, or to point them in the right direction to other Angels or what have you.

FP: Have you found that you have put together sort of syndicates of funding?

TG: No, I don't think it's reached that stage in this town. There is probably, let's say, 50 well-known Angels, and I am not going to put myself in that group, that are pretty well-healed guys down here.   And everybody hits upon them. But our idea, frankly, is to try to identify 200 more that have the economic clout to do something but for whatever reason, either they don't know how to invest, they haven't matched up with the right entrepreneur.

FP: What industries are predominantly featured in your network?

TG: You know, it's all over the place, it's high-tech, low-tech, manufacturing. What we don't have a lot of here is all intellectual service industries, where the only thing people are selling is consultancy work or management work, and that sort of stuff. Most of it has to do with some type of high-tech or tangible product, although there are some intangible products floating around.

FP: How do you find the deals that come to your network?

TG: Usually, it's word of mouth, people hear that you are a possible investor yourself or that you may know people that, if you are unwilling to invest in their particular business, that you can recommend on, just keep pushing them along the chain.

FP: Do you have a sense of what the typical size of investment is down there?

TG: Yeah. Most of the time people are looking for anywhere between 100,000 and maybe three, four, five million bucks, and the chunks down here really are, generally speaking, 25 or $50 thousand, apiece, but there are people that can go up to 100 – 200. And I'm going to say things a little different for real estate deals as opposed to what I will say to entrepreneurial deals. Real estate down here, the private investors, I mean, its just a different league, you can find well-healed people that can put in 250 or a million bucks, that's just what they do, but they don't do that with respect to start-up entrepreneurial or mid-stage entrepreneurial businesses.

FP: How many companies do you think are being invested in per year?

TG: Oh, boy! My guess is that it's - all levels of investment, okay, it's probably between 50 and 100. And what that means is you can have companies raising 100 grand that a few close friends can invest in, all the way up to the more formal deals where somebody is working through you, either an investment banker or we have a number of money brokers down here, people that go out and try to raise money from individuals, and that can get you up to 100.

FP: What do you find is the general process that Angels take in evaluating a company?

TG: I think most people try to understand the idea first, and if they understand the idea then they will go to look at the scalability of it, and then they will come back to the management that's needed to achieve that scalability.

FP: What do you hear or see as being the most important part of a business plan or an executive summary?

TG: It's probably a succinct presentation of those three things.

FP: What sort of milestones do you think people are looking for a company to have reached, and do you find that people are willing to invest in pre-revenue deals?

TG: I do find that people are <willing to invest pre-revenue>, but after the dot-com boom/bust, at least down here, what happened is those are few and far between, so it's easier to raise money, although it's always difficult. Companies have achieved some revenue level, even if it's half a million bucks, at least the idea has been proven on a very limited scale. But because the economy is changing, meaning that it's getting better, I do think that more people are considering pre-revenue companies now as investments.

FP: And how much does the competitive landscape and the size of the market that a company is operating in affect the decision to invest?

TG: I think in terms of the size of the marketplace, that is a favorable factor. I mean, if you have a relatively large marketplace, to have revenues, you can have 1% of a $100 billion marketplace, and that is significant revenues. On the other hand, 10% of a million-dollar marketplace, most people, I think, would stay away from that. And in terms of the competitor, that's a negative factor. The stronger the competition, unless you have a unique product, the big guys can always clobber you; they just have the power to do that.

FP: What do you look for in a management team?

TG: Past success would probably be number one. And if there is no particular past success with respect to raising money and having either established a profitable company or sold it to another enterprise, for example, if somebody is trying to peddle a company that is going to be involved in the semblance of PC systems, then I want to know what experience that management team has in the semblance of PC systems, where they come from. Then I think the third thing is just passion for the deal. Do these guys know everything about the marketplace? Have they committed their own financial resources to the deal? Not just passion like, say, an emotion, but passion in the sense that they got everything tied up in it so that the success of the enterprise, it will be their focus. It's not just a part-time vocation.

FP: Do you require that a company has patents?

TG: No, I don't require, but I think it would be nice if there is a patent registration, at least when that is going through the PTO.

FP: What are the milestones you look for once you make an investment?

TG: Well, the biggest milestone for me is I want to see some money coming back to the investors as soon as possible. There ought to be some sort of a return over a three-, four-, five-year period even if it is modest. Most investors are in investing to make money, and I think today more people are inclined to want to get something out of it even if it is a small amount, instead of waiting around for the big buyout to occur.

FP: Do you expect a company to come to you with a stated exit strategy?

TG: Yeah. I mean, I want to know just where they think they are going in the future. If they are saying that the only thing they are going to do is be unprofitable but gain tremendous market share, then their exit strategy is to sell out to somebody that wants to get into that marketplace and make it profitable, I would probably say, I'm not interested. Secondly, <the entrepreneur must show> what would be the extraordinary events that can really multiply your investment, and it's either selling to a larger corporation or going public.

FP: What do you expect in terms of a return on an investment?

TG: For these types of start-ups I would probably like to see my money be doubled within five years.

FP: So, what factors impact valuation, how do you value a company?

TG: There are probably two, one is financial and one is the trust in the management. The financial, it's having somebody explain to you what the marketplace is, the size of the marketplace, what they want to achieve in terms of percentage of that marketplace. What their anticipated revenues are going to be. Revenues are always the toughest thing to predict. It's the expenses you can seem to get on a much better control, and it's sort of like solving simultaneous equations because it's layered on top of one another. How are they going to generate their revenues, is always the first question. Then how do you know you're going to be at a million dollars in two years and five million dollars in three years? Who are the people you're going to go to sell the product to, who are the competitors, can they either copy you or knock you off? And then the other factor is the management, do you have this passion of management or is it going to just slavishly devote themselves to getting these revenues?

FP: Do you find that Angels want to be the lead investor or take a Board seat for their investment?

TG: More of the savvier Angel Investors want to do that stuff because, I think, they feel like most of the time the entrepreneurs are younger and so many of the Angel Investors are older, they've either had their successful businesses which have generated their money, or they have been around for a long time, and they have just picked up what is good business practices. They'd like a seat on the Board or they would like a representative of them to be on the Board so they can just look through the representative or look at first hand what is happening with the company and have an opportunity to talk to management.

FP: If you could offer an entrepreneur only one piece of advice regarding Angel Investors, what would it be?

TG: I would think that the one piece of advice would be that you are going to go through a lot of potential before you find the right investor. Who knows, you may have talked to 100 people before you get one. It's not an easy process, so I have looked at it from the entrepreneur's point of view and I am giving you the answer in terms of raising the money as opposed to what should you expect that an Angel is going to demand from you. I think that the most important thing is that you are going to have to realize you are going to have to talk to a lot of people, at least in Richmond, Virginia, to raise money.

Ellen Sandles, Executive
Director

Tri-State Private Investors
Network

New York, New York

www.angelinvestorfunding.com

ellen@angelinvestorfunding.com

Tri-State PIN
www.angelinvestorfunding.com

FP: Start by telling me a little bit about the background of the Tri-State PIN.

ES: The Tri-State PIN was formed in the year 2000. At this point, we're the longest- running Angel Investor network in the New York tri-state area, and it was formed for two purposes. One was to help start-up early-stage entrepreneurs meet investors that they would otherwise not be able to find. And two, to help the investors meet other investors so that they could invest together and do their due-diligence together, and basically, have better terms when they go to invest, because I had observed that when Angels are out there on their own, they're at a disadvantage. That was the initial founding. One of the differentiating factors about our group from the very beginning was that although we certainly do have some members who are heavy-duty technology people and like technology, we have never been a purely tech focused Angel Group, which a lot of them are. So from the very beginning we've been very open to basic businesses that are in many different industries, not just technology, not just Internet, and we still have that philosophy today. As I said, we do invest in tech companies, but we'll also look at manufacturing, consumer products, and retail. Things other groups will pretty much turn off which doesn't fit their industry specifications.

FP: What interested you personally to Angel investing?

ES: Well, I like business and I have a business background, coming from a business family. I think people who are attracted to this, in general, are entrepreneurial people to begin with, so there's an attraction to that. I also felt at the time, as I said, I knew several private investors, and I saw that when they were on their own, and not with a group, they really would lose money very quickly, and it was not an advantage to them to be out there by themselves. At the time that I formed the Tri-State PIN, there really weren't a lot of options for people. <There> just weren't a lot of opportunities in the market.

FP: Do you operate as a fund? Or do individual investors have the opportunity to go in on deals having shared due-diligence?

ES: That's really the latter, we don't operate as fund, but the investors can go in as a group having shared due-diligence and they make themselves look like a larger entity, so to say.

FP: How do you source your deals?

ES: They're sourced through a variety of ways.   At this point, we have a reputation, so that people are always registering every day at our website. So they go to the Angelinvesterfunding.com website, and there's a link there that says Tri-State Private Investors Network and they find us. They find us either through attorneys, through articles, through speaking engagements that they hear me at, doing Web research, a whole variety of ways. And sometimes our members refer deals if they find something that they like.

FP: Roughly how many companies do you invest in per year?

ES: Well, in the last year, people put money into about five different companies, but I would tell you that most Angel Groups in general are going to invest somewhere between two and four a year. That's more typical.

FP: What is the average size of investment?

ES: Again, I think our group, when they invest, they would invest anywhere between two to $400,000 on a group basis. That's also typical on the Angel Groups.

FP: When you look at business plans, what are the most important components? What sells you on a business plan?

ES: Well, the thing that's most important is that the person makes it very clear at the beginning: What market problem is it that they're solving? And that's what we try to find out, what's the problem that you're solving, and why do you think this problem needs a business solution? And then, of course, we do look at the people. What are their backgrounds? In the Angel world you don't have to be one of these star managers like the VCs might look for. We do want to see that you came out of the industry, that you have some kind of relevant background, and are not just going into something just totally new with other people's money. Of course, we look at the market size and what the cost of marketing and selling is going to be for this new product or service.

FP: What is the process for evaluating the company?

ES: The process for evaluating a company. It's funny, we just had a dinner last night, and we're starting to tweak our process a bit, so our website is going to be changed shortly. Right now, we're going to start experimenting with, and I say, "experimenting" 'cause we literally had an investment dinner last night, we're going to start experimenting with an opportunity to let entrepreneurs come in and briefly present their companies to a screening committee. Then we'll narrow down who actually gets to present at the long meeting. That's something we're going to start testing and see if people prefer that format.

FP: How long does the process take from start to finish?

ES: Well, from the time somebody submits, until the time they actually receive funding, you know, you're talking about them submitting, going through a screening process, coming in to make a presentation, right there and then alone, depending on when they get their materials in and when the meetings are, that alone can take two months. Again, that has to do with how our calendar looks. Once somebody actually gets into due-diligence, I always tell entrepreneurs that you have to allow at least three to four months for a deal to close.

FP: What sort of milestones are you looking for pre-investment and do you invest in pre-revenue deals?

ES: We're not in love with the idea of investing in pre-revenue deals unless we're going in with a very large funding source and there's enough money to lessen the risk that the company doesn't have revenues. And I would tell you that that's probably where most Angel Networks are these days; they don't have the pockets to carry non-revenue-producing companies unless they're going in with a larger VC. So if it's just an Angel opportunity, it's really best that the person has done something to initially prove or test out that they actually have a concept that's sellable. Unless they have some really extraordinary revolutionary breakthrough technology that's disruptive, and most people don't. What they really have is a marketing idea, and they really need to go out and do some marketing. Show that whatever this is, this widget that they've developed can be sold and someone can pay for it. That's really the best time to approach Angel Networks. Really not beforehand. That's probably the biggest conversation that we have with someone, where we say to them, You know, you don't really need money, what you need is to go out and sell something to someone.

FP: What are you looking for in terms of a company's management team?

ES: We want initially the team... we're not looking for a big team because the Angels don't want to support a whole slew of salaries, but we want the team - you know, if somebody started the company and he's an inventor, we would like him to be teamed with somebody's who's more a marketing person. We want to see some diversification of skills. It's very unusual for somebody who is an inventor or an engineer to also be a marketer and a salesperson. It's typically not feasible. So we like to see a diversification of skills. Now as far as financials go, a lot of these early companies don't have the financial wherewithal to bring on CFOs and full-time staff. One of our sponsors is a company called Gellar & Company, and they provide outsourced financial support for emerging companies, so we recommend our entrepreneurs for outsourced financial help use Gellar & Company. The same thing comes with technology development. Another one of our sponsors is a company called Ternary Software. Most early-stage companies cannot afford full-time IT staff, so Ternary Software can fulfil that role on an outsourced basis and working with emerging companies. And that's fine for us. If companies are using these outside entities to help them, that's fine.

FP: Do you require a company have patents?

ES: Well... If you don't have patents, now I don't want to say that's a requirement, but we need to - let's say nothing is really that patentable, then we need to understand where your barrier-to-entry is going to be. What are you going to do to sustain the business so that it has a place in the market before others can copy it?

FP: How much do you expect management to understand the competitive landscape?

ES: They have to understand the competitive landscape; they really do, that's very important! It's very, very important that they've thought that out and researched it.   What we don't want to hear is that there is no competition. You're competing against the status quo.

FP: What's the expected time horizon to a liquidity event and what's your general expectation in terms of ROI?

ES: Usually, most investors are looking for or expecting that they're going to be in the company at least anywhere from three to five years, and most investors for this early stage-risk will tell you they're looking for 10 times their money, depending how early the company is.

FP: Now, does Tri-State PIN often take the position of lead investor? How have term sheets changed since the bubble?

ES: Sometimes we take the position of lead investor, I wouldn't say always; I wouldn't say often, it varies. Sometimes the Angel groups trade off who takes the lead on the deal. Sometimes if there's a VC leading the deal, Angel Groups will join those deals. I mean up to the very early-stage VCs, not your typical larger VCs. Sometimes we do.

As far as how term sheets have changed, well, I think that they've changed in the sense that, you know, there were all these incredible valuations that people would just get off the bat years ago without anyone questioning because there was always an assumption that someone else would come in with more money and pay more, and that's just not the case these days. Valuations are more tightly controlled, and really once you get to Angel world, valuations tend to be anywhere from one to four million.

FP: What factors impact valuation? How do you get to a number?

ES: Usually, the investors get to it and it's pretty much based on what their feelings are. You know, there aren't scientific ways to value early-stage companies, because they haven't been around long enough and they don't have enough historicals. So a company that has some sales traction and has more sales traction than, say, another company will probably get a higher valuation than the other company. But really, it's the number the investors feel comfortable with.

FP: If you could offer an entrepreneur only one piece of advice regarding Angel Investors, what would it be?

ES: My piece of advice would be to really show that you have a business before going out to raise money. I think that's where most people really stumble. I mean, we had a meeting the other day with somebody and he, as an individual, was selling something, but he hadn't shown that other people could sell what he was proposing, and that's what was critical to his business. That other people sell this thing he developed. So he went looking for money before showing that other people can actually sell what he developed, and so, therefore, he is going to get delayed. That is really the problem that people make, they go out and they're still too early. You really have to show that you can sell something. If your model is: "I developed something and other people are going to sell it and that's how I'm going to make my revenues," then show us that you've brought on one or two other people that can sell it. Prove the concept. Yes, proof of concept, I would say, is a very big one!

Robert Robinson
University of Hawaii Angels
Honolulu, Hawaii
http://hawaiiangels.org
info@hawaiiangels.org
808-447-9372

**University of
Hawaii Angels**

FP: How did you become involved with Angel Investing, what's your background?

RR: Okay. Well, I'm a business school professor and I - a couple of years ago I wrote a book on Angel investing called <u>Angel Investing,</u> and it was really the first sort of definitive study of Angel Investing. And I wrote it with a post doc from Oxford, this was back when I was at Harvard Business School. We wrote this book together, it's still available, you can see it on Amazon. So that's my book, and I'm not sure how much information you want on how I got involved with that, but basically, I've been studying business and negotiations. And then in the '90s a lot of my students were getting involved in these start-ups, and so I started studying what they were doing, and I became very interested in the issue of entrepreneurship, per se, and basically the early-stage funding because it seemed like all of my students... there was kind of a hard step in getting the first infusion of capital. So I wanted to learn more about who did that kind of investing. It seemed like sort of institutional capital providers were not doing that, and that's where I sort of really learned about Angel Investing and so on. A couple of years ago, I took this job in Hawaii. They were just starting an entrepreneurship center here and they were looking for a director, and when I was thinking of taking the job, I said to them that one of my priorities, if I take this job, will be to establish an Angel Investing Network in Honolulu because there really is not one currently. A lot of people apparently have talked about it over the years but nobody had taken action to form a group. The University seemed like neutral ground for groups to meet and so on, so that's what we did with the help of some of the local business people. In February of 2002, so almost three years ago now, we started UH Angels.

FP: How many Angels are in the group?

RR: We have about 40 paid members, and then we have, well, we have a mailing list of about 120 people who are not members who want to stay in touch with what we are doing, and sort of what you might think of as occasional members, and if they come, we just charge them for the lunch. If they come to us and we tell them that they have to join. So we have 40 members who pay the 500 bucks per-year annual fee, which is really quite reasonable, actually, because they get a lunch and so on, once a month. And because we're with the University and so on, we're not in it for any profit, and we use any surplus we have for educational events or bringing in speakers or so on. Once we bought a laptop, that kind of thing.

FP: Are you a network of Angels or is there also a fund connected to the group?

RR: We are solely a network. I would like to eventually get to the point of having a fund, but in my studies that seems to be something that comes with maturity, and we're not there yet. I think that we're closer than we were before, but we do not have a fund at this time.

FP: What industries do you find the Angels are typically investing in?

RR: Well, my group of Angels is actually - probably because of just the way we formed and so on, in my group of Angels, we're primarily interested in high-tech, and we've done biotechnology deals, we've done software deals, nanotechnology deals. We also have in Hawaii a strong interest in marine agriculture and the things related to marine agriculture, basically. So, life sciences are a strong interest here in Hawaii, as well as sort of marine sciences.

FP: Roughly how many companies have you found that the group is investing in per year?

RR: It's actually timely that you called us because I just did my summary, and I got my members to give me information just a couple of weeks ago. Since 2002, in the three years we've been in business, we've done 20 deals, so we're quite active. We've by far had our best year last year, and I think we did 11 deals last year.

FP: What have you found is the average size of an investment?

RR: As a group or as individuals? As a group, we've been averaging - the average has been creeping up, but we've been averaging slightly more than 250,000 a deal. So it's about 260 now. As individuals, it's meaningful because there are larger investments and some much smaller ones, so we get people who do 25 and we get people who do 300 kind of thing. I would say that sort of the median investment is probably like $50,000 per Angel per investment.

FP: How does the group source its deals?

RR: We basically look at everything that comes in over the transom because we're more or less the only game in town. We've had a fair amount of publicity, and also because of the University connection, people regard us as being reasonable. We don't charge a fee or anything for the presenter, so pretty much anybody can come and talk to us, so we get stuff coming in over the transom and, of course, we prefer the personal referrals. A number of our members are, in fact, entrepreneurs who presented, and a couple of them have gotten funded and that definitely helps. If nobody knows these people at all, well, Hawaii is a very small place and so that's kind of a bad sign. Certainly, if somebody - if we don't happen to know somebody at the beginning, we will ask around and we can pretty soon find out who knows them.

FP: Is part of the mission of the group that you look only at local companies?

RR: It's difficult because of where we are, but we've had people with Hawaii connections look to raise part of their money here, but they are actually on the Mainland. We've had one or two venture capitalists who have homes here that have brought us deals that are already about 85% funded on the Mainland and we've chipped in some money. You know, it sort of has to make sense because I think nobody here really wants to be trying to monitor an investment in New York or something if there are no connections, but we don't have a policy against it.

FP: What's the process by which companies get evaluated?

RR: We have a screening process. We don't have a formal checklist or a formal set of criteria. We do give them some information on what we're looking for and then we have a screening. We generally have a screening meeting about once a month in addition to the regular meeting where we ask people to come. For example, on Thursday of this week we're having two or three companies come by and sort of talk us through their model and their presentation. Then, one of a couple of things will happen. Either we'll say, "Yeah, this looks great, we'd like to get you in for a meeting" or we'll say well, "You know, we think it needs some work along with this and this – dimensions." We'll assign one of the executive members to work and liaise with the companies on that and then when they say these guys re-worked their business plan or their financials or whatever we've said, then we may have them back again, or we may just say, All right, let's schedule you in for a presentation. It's relatively informal, but we have usually about seven or eight members of the executive at any screening meeting so they get a pretty thorough scrubbing and then we go from there.

FP: How long does the screening process take and then how long would the due- diligence process take on average?

RR: Well, you know, we don't do due-diligence until after the presentation if there are people interested in investing. The actual screening process, which would include asking around about these people and what they know and so on, typically it takes a couple of weeks. You know, the actual meeting may only be about an hour but, you know, it's just having people review the executive summary and the business plan and asking around. Generally takes not too long. I mean, how long does it actively take? A week or two. It often takes longer, but nobody's trying to take longer. Then with the due-diligence, after the presentation, if people are interested in investing then we go into due- diligence mode which is driven by whichever member wants to take the lead on that. So that can, I would say that it typically takes about three weeks, but we've certainly had cases where it's taken a lot longer. And we've also catered to the fact that this is a growing concern with substantially credible people involved. We've done it shorter but I would say three weeks is about average.

FP: What do you consider the most important component of a business plan or executive summary?

RR: Well, a couple of things. One is the usual things that most people look for which is that we want to see if the business makes sense from the point of view of an Angel Investor. Is there a well-thought-through plan, is the team well put together that looks like they know what they are doing, is there an exit here for investors. I think it's very important, we don't like plans that don't have an exit or have too high a valuation. We know that the next round will come from venture fund capital, we see markets forming up again so we have to moderate then. Then I think we have one additional criterion which is probably unique to us, which is, does this make sense in Hawaii, because there's certain things that don't make a whole lot of sense in Hawaii, like, you know, heavy manufacturing, for example, and why would this succeed in Hawaii. That's a question we ask quite straight.

FP: What sort of milestones do you typically look for pre-investment and do you look at pre-revenue deals?

RR: Oh, yeah, we absolutely look at pre-revenue deals although clearly, one of the more important milestones that we would like to see is that they do have customer interest, you know. We would like to see product and we'd like to see the thing being put together. We'd also like to - our preference is to see people working full-time on the business rather than keeping their day job and just doing this as they can. We like to see product, so if it's a prototype that is much better than just being a bunch of drawings. Obviously, if there is a product that's already in service with a potential client or something, that's even better. Customer testimonials are good, you know, that sort of thing.

FP: What do you look for in a management team? Many investors say that is a critical factor.

RR: Yes. Yes, I think that's absolutely true. I think we all believe that. From my point of view, I would like to see entrepreneurs doing it not for the first time. I mean, everyone has to start somewhere, but we much prefer to see someone who is making his or her third business. That's absolutely critical. And then, you know, obviously, have the fleshed out the necessary skills of the business. The fact that someone's your college roommate doesn't necessarily mean that they have complimentary skills. We don't want everyone to have the same skills, so depending on what we think the core needs of the business are, if they are lacking that, then we have a serious talk with them. It's not necessarily a disqualifier, but we say to them, you know, Look, if you get some money from us, the first thing you need to do is go out and hire a marketing person or something like that. And so we're concerned about that.

FP: How do the competitive landscape and the size of the market impact an Angel's decision to invest?

RR: Well, obviously, we're very sensitive to that in Hawaii here because we don't want to start - there's no point in starting a little business in Hawaii that turns out it can't spread beyond Hawaii because it's locked by major national and international competitors.   Obviously, because we're mostly in the tech space, we're very concerned that there would be a market out there that's really interested in a little local business even though they may be profitable in their own right.   Most of my guys are looking at this as traditional venture investors – we're very concerned, being so isolated in Hawaii, that we may be overlooking major competitive assets that are taking place elsewhere. So that's probably one of the things that we look at closely.

FP: What kind of protections do you require for intellectual property?

RR: Well, we definitely like to see patents pending in the business plan. It's one of those things that... It's kind of a necessary but not a sufficient kind of thing to have. If they haven't protected intellectual property then, obviously, it's really not a very good situation.   If they have protected intellectual property, they still might not actually have protections that are worth anything, but at least they've done what they are supposed to do. Two of our members are actually intellectual property attorneys and so they're pretty strong on that, so we look into that pretty carefully. I mean, we've done some deals that are premised more on trade secrets than on IP. That's fine, too, as long as it's a good secret that is not readily reverse engineered or anything. That can work, as well.

FP: Once you actually make an investment, what kind of milestones do you expect the company to reach from that investment?

RR: Well, it depends very much on the investment. I mean, for the most part we are not the lead investors in these deals and so we don't have that much say over what the strategic direction of the company is going forward. But clearly, if we are investing in a business that doesn't project needing more capital beyond the current round of investment, we like to see them moving to a positive response and then moving to some sort of exit strategy that entails usually acquisition. If we're investing in a business where there are subsequent rounds of investment required, we do look very carefully at what the milestones are that are projected, and what is necessary to track those second rounds of capital, and we track that pretty carefully. But those can vary from getting your full release of your product or signing up a certain number of customers, you know, whatever... So, we monitor those, but we don't have a specific set of requirements.

FP: Do you find that Angels take lead investor positions and seats on Boards of Directors?

RR: I think initially, especially when there is an A round, it is quite typical for Angels to take a Board seat and, you know, one of the things I have to do constantly is decline to take Board seats because I run this group. They sort of figure I should be on the board but usually I say, No, no, no. You know, the person who invests money should be on the board because otherwise I'd be on 20 boards, and that's just not doable.

Initially, we had no interest in being the lead investors because as a group, I mean, I had more experience than most of them, the group as a whole had very little experience with term sheets or how to negotiate as a lead. And I think, as time has passed, we've gotten more comfortable with that so we sort of - each year we've gotten more senior in our position in a lot of these rounds and, in fact, we've just recently done one or two deals where it looks like - they're not quite done yet, but it looks like we'll be the lead investors. In my experience and in my research, I mean senior groups like Boston Common Angels, they do lead all of the time, so it depends on your size, I think, and, you know, your maturity.

FP: What about term sheets, how have they changed since the bubble?

RR: I guess, you know, there's been, I guess, a number of changes. Many of the changes have more to do with the protection of the investor in the event that events go bad. During the bubble, it was just an assumption that people were going to go charging through to some sort of liquidity event at great speed. I mean, investors are much less interested in getting options than they are in getting, if they can, some sort of interest component to the investment so that they can get some of their money out.

FP: More of a convertible note?

RR: Yeah, a convertible note type of deal. I'm seeing a fair amount of that. Definitely valuation has become more conservative. The process of valuation is just much, much more realistic than it was during the bubble. There are probably other things that I could put my finger on if I tried, but those are the ones that occur to me right now.

FP: What factors are driving valuations now, especially in these early-stage companies?

RR: Right. Well, you know, as always there's an aspect of comparables involved which is, someone was telling me, for example, someone who spends their time in Hawaii and on the West Coast, basically A rounds, pre-money between two and four million dollars is typical, and it doesn't really matter what kind of business you are in. That is certainly true here, too. There's just this sort of paradigm that you don't try and put a high valuation on, then the market will bear. But then, you know, also there's things like, have they achieved any kind of revenue flow yet, and if they have, it definitely bumps their valuation up. I would say having customers and actually having cash flow is probably the two biggest things that will draw valuation up at the moment. Otherwise, it doesn't really matter.

FP: What have you found is the expected time horizon to exit, and what do you think people are thinking of in terms of ROI?

RR: Yeah. What we really sort of tell our prospective investors and also the prospective presenters is that as a group, we're looking for three to 5X over three to five years. That's sort of our mantra, three to 5X over three to five years. Of course, we're all hoping for the big hits, the 10X the 50X. But, realistically speaking, if you can get a 3X in three years or a 5X in five years, I think that's pretty decent. So that's pretty much what we're shooting for.

FP: Do you counsel Angels to invest only in technologies that they have previous experience in?

RR: Well, yes, I do. What I tell people when they join is that there are no requirements that they invest immediately. There's actually no requirement that they invest, but the sort of expectation is that they will, but we tell them to take their time, get comfortable, don't go rushing into a deal that you don't know anything about. And ideally, look for something that you know something about. That's the best kind of advice we can give you. We do explicitly coach them about that.

FP: If you could offer an entrepreneur only one piece of advice regarding a seed round and Angel Investors, what would it be?

RR: I would say probably - well it's a two-part piece of advice, I would say, Don't get too hung up on valuation because at the end of the day it doesn't matter as much as you think it does. And secondly, look for value-added investors. Don't just take anybody's money if you have the option. Look for people who can bring expertise and contacts and, you know, background and so on that will actually enhance your business as opposed to people who can just write you a check. Obviously, if you need the money, you need the money, but if you have the choice, look for value-added investors.

FEATURED ANGEL INTERVIEW

Denis Coleman, Angel
Investor
Band of Angels, LLC
Menlo Park, California
www.bandangels.com
info@bandangels.com

FP: You've been part of Band of Angels for awhile?

DC: Yeah, I think it was about 1997 – 1998, for about six or seven years. I wasn't quite there at the beginning.

FP: So, tell me a little bit about your background. How did you get interested in Angel Investing?

DC: I guess it was just something to do. I was a founder of several companies and I guess I didn't want a full-time job. The opportunities came to me that sort of looked interesting, so I sort of got involved quite often with the companies or I had an idea of my own and started a company. It's always better to have someone else's money in it along with yours.

FP: Are there specific industries in which you invest?

DC: I've sort of invested into a whole bunch of different things, from biotech to software to Internet to a High-Speed Ferry Service in Hawaii.

FP: How do you find your deals?

DC: You know, deals come to me, the ones that come to the Band dinner. And other than that, people just sort of call me up with deals, so I really don't do any looking, they just find their way to me.

FP: What's the typical size of your investment?

DC: The largest is 200, and 25 is usually the minimum. So probably 25 to 75 is the range.   You got to keep in mind that when you make investments, you have to be prepared to put that much money down again for the next round.

FP: How many investments do you hold?

DC: Well, including ones that have gone public, I think it's about 13 or 14.

FP: Okay, roughly how many companies do you invest in per year?

DC: You know, my goal is three, but last year was six. I hate saying no – they all look nice to me. That's why the Band is tough, you see so many deals and you have to say no so many times. This is a good exercise.

FP: What tends to be your process for evaluating the company?

DC: The biggest thing is meeting with the principles that are making it happen. It has to be a product that I believe in, and preferably one that I would like to use. In the medical area, that's a little bit more difficult because you sort of like to not use some of these things. If you did need them, that would be valuable. So, it's basically - I like growth markets. As a matter of fact, that is pretty much all I will invest in, something that has a lot of growth, because it's too hard to displace existing people. So it has to be a new product, new technology that has some sort of big wave of change, and it's my feeling that the people are really the most important thing and meeting with them.

FP: What do you look for in a management team?

DC: The most important thing is related experience. You know, another criterion for me is that they either have, or are willing to have, a reasonable equity structure. Quite often, the equity in these very early deals has not been thought out or properly documented, and in many cases, it's what I consider a range of fairness. Some people are willing to sort that out immediately and others are resistant, and if they are resistant then I don't like a deal. It's just too hard to get everything else sorted out if there isn't a fundamental belief in the fairness of the equity.

FP: When you look at a business plan, what are the key factors there that you are looking for?

DC: You usually don't see these long business plans. You usually see two-page summaries here. It has to be some value to the market that I believe in that they can articulate in a reasonable length of time. You know, if the thing is sort of meandering and talks all about the background of the people, a lot of which isn't relevant, then that's a bad indication to me that they can't communicate what they're going to do in their value proposition. You know, briefly. They also have to tell me what they're going to do, not just "We're going to bring the following benefits," and then it takes them forever to get around to telling you what the product is going to be that they are going to sell. The projections have to be somewhat reasonable. These things are often sort of off the wall and a lot of it's done without data, but one has to come up with something that is reasonable.

FP: Now, do you invest in pre-revenue deals?

DC: Yes. Definitely.

FP: So, when you are looking at those deals, what sort of milestones are you looking for the company to have accomplished?

DC: Well, the big one is what I call the "free test." If the company is pre-revenue and the product isn't completed or maybe it is only just designed, what I like to see is that people have the contacts and can point to somebody, and maybe it's their uncle or their friend or their former boss or someone who can say, "Jeez, when this is done, I may not be willing to pay, but I'm sure going to use this." So, if one cannot see that much demand, then it's probably not a good idea.

FP: What sort of valuations do you look for? Does a company have to have a minimum market size for you to invest?

DC: You know, I like to invest in a company where the pre-money is less than two million dollars. So, not to be greedy here, but if you don't go for 10-to-1 returns, you're not going to get very far these days, because things don't always work out. What's the company need for a market to be worth 20, 30, 40 million dollars. So, 50 million market size that they could get a good piece of and they have to come up with some reasonable numbers to support that. You know, there are so many labs; we can get such and such a percentage of them at such and such a price. So, yeah, the basic numbers should be there, and they should've thought about who's going to use this thing to come up with those numbers and done enough basic research. It doesn't take long these days with the Internet to come up with basic numbers.

FP: What do you expect them to know about the competitive landscape of their industry?

DC: Well, a lot. If they don't know who the major players are, then that makes me real nervous. It's just not that hard to find out these days. Basically, if I ask about the competitors and I see that there's this one they didn't mention, then that is a real problem.

FP: Do you require that companies have patents or some sort of protection of IP?

DC: You know, these days, everybody says, We are applying for patents. And it takes so long to get them, nobody - you know, not that many people at this early stage have the patents. Just because somebody submits an application, you don't know whether or not it's going to be approved or whether it's going to be of economic significance. You know, it's nice to see, but certainly in the Internet space people say they are applying for all of these patents, and I think being a first mover and having the best product is the issue, and often the patents are not important at all.

FP: When you make an investment, what do you then expect the next milestones to be for that capital?

DC: Well, the next milestone is either the next round of investment or cash flow breakeven. So, in order to get to that next round of investment, they have to achieve certain goals. You know, getting the product working, getting endorsement from customers, getting a sales pipeline going. The question you have to ask is, Who is going to be putting in the next round of investment, and What are their criteria, so one may sit and look at what the venture capitalist is going to be saying about this.

FP: So, getting to that next revenue target is critical?

DC: Yes.

FP: What factors impact your valuation?

DC: One thing is how much work has really been put into it. How much have they done. If somebody has sat down on a few weekends and written up a two-page summary and said, "This is worth a million and a half dollars," well, you know, it better be an idea I believe in, otherwise it just isn't worth that much, I don't think. You know, it depends on the backgrounds of the individuals. If it's somebody who has had significant achievements in the past and knows what they are doing, and has the contacts here to hire a good team cheap, then that's worth a lot. It's hard to base a valuation on projected sales of 75 million in four or five years from now. It's more what's been done, who are the people, who can they attract, and do I basically believe that the market is there.

FP: So it's a little more intangible than just sort of comparables and discounting cash flows and that sort of thing?

DC: Yeah. I just don't see how you can do a discounted cash flow at this stage because it's so uncertain.

FP: How long do you anticipate before liquidity event when you make an investment?

DC: Four years.

FP: How long does the due-diligence process generally take?

DC: Two to four weeks. That's the advantage here of the Angel, in my case anyway. A quick decision. I also like to think, you know, I make a quick decision, I like to see a reasonable valuation, and if I don't like a deal, I like to think that I tell people nicely something that will be useful so that they can answer some of the questions and find funding elsewhere, because they have an honest answer as to where the weaknesses are from an investor's standpoint.

FP: That means just having you look at a company means you add value even if you don't invest. Every entrepreneur who encounters you is lucky then.

DC: Well, I'd like to think that if they have a terrible executive summary here and I tell them why it's terrible and I'm not going to invest, then maybe it's not the executive summary, maybe it's just that I don't like the space for some reason, or I don't like them for some reason. The fact that I've gone through and told them what I think is wrong with their executive summary will prove useful to them. If they are not listening, then maybe it won't. But I often get thank-yous for being critical in a nice way.

FP: If you could offer an entrepreneur only one piece of advice regarding a seed round and Angel Investors, what would it be?

DC: I think the advice is that any investment round needs a lead, and your lead is probably going to be somebody you know. So, when you sit down with an idea, you make a list of everybody that you know who might be the lead investor, and just keep in mind that getting that person to stand forward, who has some reputation as an investor or domain knowledge in the field, is going to be critical. People like to see progress, so when you can talk to a dozen people, one of whom might be your champion, I would say, do that sooner rather than later so that three months later when you've really gotten farther with it you can go back to them and they'll see the progress you've made in the last three months, and they'll say, "Hey, this is really moving, I like that. This guy's doing something."

FP: Do you actually expect to see friends and family money in an investment before you want to invest yourself?

DC: Well, you've got to be very careful about family money because sometimes it comes in without knowledge. Yeah, I mean, I like to see that the entrepreneur has worked with someone who believes in them enough to put some cash down. That's a good sign. And it's certainly a red flag if no one is willing to do that.

I also like to see what they are going to pay themselves. You know, we've seen some real surprises there. It seems like a rude question, it almost sounds like a relative here who wants to know what everybody in the family makes and is sort of willing to ask. To sit down with someone and look them in the eye and say, "How much are you going to make?" You got to do it. How they answer that question is important because if the guy is going to lead a company, he's got to be good at handling that sort of thing.

Angel Investor Contacts (Volume 1)

Nicola Foreman, Deal Manager
Band of Angels Management, LLC
Menlo Park, California
www.bandangels.com
info@bandangels.com

Denis Coleman, Angel Investor
Band of Angels Management, LLC
Menlo Park, California
www.bandangels.com
info@bandangels.com

Richard Anders, Managing Director & Founder
Mass Medical Angels
Boston, MA
www.massmedangels.com
info@massmedicalangels.com

Karen Griffith Gryga, Executive Director
The Mid-Atlantic Angel Group Fund
Philadelphia, Pennsylvania
www.magfund.com
karen@sep.benfranklin.org
215-972-6700 x3061

Dee Harris, President
Arizona Angels
2415 E. Camelback Road, Suite 700, Phoenix, AZ 85016
www.arizonaangels.com
dharris@arizona-angels.org

Paul Sciabica
New York Angels
New York, New York
www.newyorkangels.com
info@newyorkangels.com
212-459-7388

Lou Anne Flanders-Stec, Fund Executive
Piedmont Angel Network
Greensboro, North Carolina
www.piedmontangelnetwork.com
lafstec@piedmontangelnetwork.com
336-235-0941

Tom Grant
The Richmond Venture Forum
Richmond, Virginia
www.ventureclub.com
tom.grant@troutmansanders.com
804-267-3370

Ellen Sandles, Executive Director
Tri-State Private Investors Network
New York, New York
www.angelinvestorfunding.com
ellen@angelinvestorfunding.com

Robert Robinson
University of Hawaii Angels
Honolulu, Hawaii
http://hawaiiangels.org
info@hawaiiangels.org
808-447-9372

Bonus: Contacts for Other Angel Groups across the Country

Pasadena Angels
http://www.pasadenaangels.com/
Pasadena, CA
info@pasadenaangels.com

Sacramento Angels
http://www.pasadenaangels.com
PO Box 1141, Roseville, CA 95678
selections@sacangels.org

Rockies Venture Club
http://www.rockiesventureclub.org/home/index.php
1805 S. Bellaire Street, Suite 480, Denver, Colorado 80222
303-831-4174

Angel Investor Forum
http://www.angelinvestorforum.com
1780 Main St, Glastonbury, CT 06033
rbabcock@angelinvestorforum.com
860-430-1257

Washington Dinner Club
http://www.washingtondinnerclub.com
Washington, DC
John@NewVantageGroup.Com

Emergent Growth Fund
http://www.emergentgrowth.com
101 SE 2nd Place, Suite 201C, Gainesville, FL 32601
interest@emergentgrowth.com
352-335-3021

Atlanta Technology Angels
http://www.angelatlanta.com
75 5th Street, NW, Suite 325, Atlanta, GA 30308
director@angelatlanta.com

Northwest Angel Network Inc
http://www.theangelpeople.com/
3350 Americana Terrace, Suite 350, Boise, Idaho 83706
info@theangelpeople.com
208-424-8438

Bi-State Investment Group
http://www.kcbig.com/
Lenexa, KS
joe@joekessinger.com

Louisiana Angel Network
http://www.louisianaangelnetwork.com
Baton Rouge, LA   225-612-2154

Launchpad Venture Group
http://www.launchpadventuregroup.com
Wellesley, MA
manager@launchpadventuregroup.com

River Valley Investors
http://www.rivervalleyinvestors.com
PO Box 897 South Hadley, MA 01075
joseph@rivervalleyinvestors.com
413-585-9692

Walnut Venture Associates
http://www.walnutventures.com/site
Wellesley Hills, MA
info@walnutentures.com

Chesapeake Emerging Opportunities Club
http://www.ceopportunities.com
9256 Bendix Road, Suite 300, Columbia, MD 21045
tarag@ecapitalllc.com
443-367-0101

Grand Angels
http://www.grandangels.org
10720 Adams Street, Holland, MI 491423
info@grandangels.org   616-546-4559

Atlantis Group
http://www.theatlantisgroup.net
2530 Meridian Parkway 3rd Floor, Durham, NC 27713
info@TheAtlantisGroup.net
919-806-4340

eCoast Angels
http://www.ecoast.org/venturecapital.cfm
P.O. Box 239, 500 Market Street, Portsmouth, NH 03802-0239
ecoastangels@comcast.net   603-436-3988

Jumpstart New Jersey Angel Network
http://www.jumpstartnj.com
1001 Briggs Road, Suite 280, Mt. Laurel, NJ 08054
info@jumpstartnj.com
856-813-1440

New Mexico Private Investors
http://www.nmprivateinvestors.com
1155 University Blvd SE, Albuquerque, NM 87106
jchavez@nmangels.com
505-843-4206

Tech Valley Angel Network
http://www.techvalleyangels.com
63 State Street, Albany, NY 12207
info@techvalleyangels.com
518-465-8975

Core Network
http://www.core-network.org
101 Main Street, Toledo, OH 43605
info@core-network.org
419-697-9696

Alliance of Angels
http://www.allianceofangels.com
Rainier Tower Building, 1301 Fifth Avenue, Suite 2500, Seattle, WA 98101
info@allianceofangels.com
206-389-7258

Enterprise Oklahoma Venture Fund

http://www.i2e.org

Presbyterian Health Foundation Research Park, 840 Research Pkwy, Ste 250, OKC, OK 73104   twalker@i2E.org

405-235-2305

Portland Angel Network

http://www.oen.org

309 SW Sixth Ave, Suite 212, Portland, Oregon 97204

PAN@oef.org   503-222-2270

Lancaster Angel Network

http://www.venture-forum.org/AngelList.html

c/o Wellspring FV LLC, 128 East Grant Street, Fourth Floor, Lancaster, PA 17602

mas@wellspringfv.com

717-293-5151

Utah Angels

http://www.utahangels.org

Salt Lake City, UT

info@utahangels.org

Charleston Angel Partners

http://www.chapsc.com

Charelston, SC

Andrea@charlestonAngels.com   843-881-5623

Beacon Angels

http://beaconangels.com

Boston, MA

candidates@beaconangels.com

Nashville Capital Network
http://www.nashvillecapital.com
40 Burton Hills Blvd, Suite 320, Nashville, TN 37215
schambless@nashvillecapital.com
615-322-9016

Houston Angel Network
http://www.houstonangelnetwork.org
Houston, TX
kmarathi@houstonangelnetwork.org   832-476-9291

Southwest Pennsylvania Angel Network
http://www.innovationworks.org/span/index.jsp
Innovation Works, 2000 Technology Drive Suite 250, Pittsburgh, PA 15219-3109
mharbaugh@innovationworks.org
412-681-1520

North Country Angels
http://www.northcountryangels.com
Vermont
wainwright@northcountryangels.com

Vegas Valley Angels
http://www.vegasvalleyangels.angelgroups.net
PO Box 1234, Las Vegas, NV 8128
info@vegasvalleyangels.com

Marquette University Golden Angels Network
http://mukohlercenter.org/pages/Welcome/Golden_Angels/
P.O. Box 1881, Milwaukee, WI 53201-1881
tim.keane@marquette.edu   414-288-5722

Ariel Savannah Angel Partners
http://www.savannahangelpartners.com
Savannah, GA
rwenig1@earthlink.net
843-342-9642

Centennial Investors
http://centennialinvestors.com
300 S. Providence Rd, Columbia, MO 65203-1016
info@centennialinvestors.com
573-884-0467

Golden Seeds
http://www.goldenseeds.com
New York, NY & Boston, MA
1-888-629-6774

Granite Stage Angels
http://granitestateangels.com
Bristol, New Hampshire
info@granitestateangels.com

Life Science Angels
http://www.lifescienceangels.com
Palo Alto, CA
anngaddy@sbcglobal.net

ARC Angel Fund
http://www.ARCAngelFund.com
885 3rd Ave, 20th FL
New York, NY 10022

Be sure to read:

How To Raise Your First Million Dollars From Angel Investors Volume 2, with even more Angel Investor Interviews and Another Directory of Angel Groups, available at www.FundingPost.com

ISBN 978-0-578-02627-5

www.FundingPost.com

www.ingramcontent.com/pod-product-compliance
Lightning Source LLC
Chambersburg PA
CBHW031813190326
41518CB00006B/323